Testimonials

Here are some of the things our members from The Best 90 Days Ever membership have said about the group.

'The Best 90 Days Ever has truly transformed my business for the better. As a part-time freelancer I'm often strapped for time, but Hannah's daily prompts in weekly themes have enabled me to work on so many parts of my business in an easy and fun way. My business now feels so much more put together and slick. It's amazing to see how much of an impact completing a 10–30-minute prompt can have on growing your business in the long run.'

Sioned – Mwydro, www.mwydro.com

'Being a member of the Best 90 Days has revolutionized marketing for me. It's given me so many quick and easy tips that are helping me to get my business out there, pushing me to do a lot of things I would never have otherwise done. The support in the Facebook group is amazing. But the best bit is being able to dip in and out as and when I need to. If I don't have time to do the prompts when they're live, I just save them and go back to them when I've got time.'

Suzy – Wish Freelance Writing, www.wishfreelancewriting.com

'Hannah's ideas and how she works is incredible; she sees inspiration in everything. Her 10-minute marketing is genius, and do-able for everyone, along with this, her motivation is contagious. Her expertise and fantastic tips on breaking content down has made me tick things off my to-do list that have been building up for a very long time. I'm looking forward to working more with Hannah and to see what other gems she will bring out!'

Rhodd – Rhodd Hughes, Personal Training

HANNAH ISTED

The Best 90 Days Ever

How **10-minute marketing** can transform your business one day at a time

First published in Great Britain by Practical Inspiration Publishing, 2024

© Hannah Isted, 2024

The moral rights of the author have been asserted

ISBN   9781788605311   (PB print)
        9781788605816   (HB print)
        9781788605335   (epub)
        9781788605328   (mobi)

Every effort has been made to trace copyright holders and to obtain their permission for the use of copyright material. The publisher apologizes for any errors or omissions and would be grateful if notified of any corrections that should be incorporated in future reprints or editions of this book.

Want to bulk-buy copies of this book for your team and colleagues? We can customize the content and co-brand *The Best 90 Days Ever* to suit your business's needs.

Please email info@practicalinspiration.com for more details.

Practical Inspiration
Publishing

Contents

Introduction

Welcome to *The Best 90 Days Ever*! If you picked up this book then I'm guessing you want to get better at marketing your business. Well, you're in the right place.

I started The Best 90 Days Ever as an online marketing membership for small business owners and since then it has grown into an amazing community of people.

I've used everything I've learnt from years of working in marketing to try and make social media, sales and everything in between accessible, enjoyable and most importantly, quick! It hasn't always been this way, so let's go back a few years and I'll tell you where it all began.

After university, I started working in social media and PR. I remember watching the long-term employee awards at work one day and knowing that wasn't for me. The company was great, but I didn't want to work there for 25 years, I wanted to work for myself. I had always known that I wanted to run my own business, I just hadn't been brave enough to take the leap.

A few months later I handed in my notice and my employers were brilliant. The team supported me starting my own social media business and I even took them on as one of my first clients and continued working on projects with them.

In 2018 I moved to Barry in South Wales (that's a story for another day!) where I met my now husband, Tom. We started a digital magazine called Barry Magazine, organized the first ever Barry Pride event and realized we were actually very good at working together.

As a social media manager, I work with businesses who are struggling with their marketing. I love collaborating with them, but I started realizing that for many businesses, it didn't make sense to hire a social media manager. They could easily do it themselves if they just knew how.

There needed to be a way of teaching business owners how to be their own social media manager, without taking up all of their valuable time. Most business owners didn't sign up to become marketing experts as well.

We are all busy and already spending a lot of time in front of our laptops and phones. Who wants to spend even more time writing blogs for their website and recording videos? I know I'd rather be out walking the dogs on the beach than spending an extra hour working on a reel.

But the problem is, your audience does want to know more about YOU. They want to see behind the scenes content, they want to know your opinions about your industry, they want you to share your tips and advice with them.

When it comes to marketing I don't believe that the more time you spend the better the results will be.

There will (nearly) always be someone else that has a similar product or offer to you. The difference is that they don't have you. Your viewpoint makes you unique and that's something to be celebrated! Showing up on social media as yourself can be the secret weapon for your brand and I promise you that it doesn't need to take all day.

So many factors go into creating a piece of great content and time is just one of them. You only have to be on TikTok for 5 minutes to see videos with millions of views that have taken 30 seconds to record.

I started challenging myself to get my work done in a shorter time and, fast forward a couple of years, my marketing membership The Best 90 Days Ever was born.

This book is based on the membership that changed the way I see marketing and teaches you how to promote your business every single day for just 10 minutes at a time. Each week we have a different theme with seven daily prompts for you to complete. They are fast, fun and should help you forget that marketing used to feel like a chore.

I'll show you the daily marketing tasks hundreds of business owners have used to grow their audience and promote their products and services, with examples of how you could use this advice yourself to transform your business too in just 10 minutes at a time.

I know some of us feel like we don't have time for marketing, but if you can give me 10 minutes a day for the next 3 months, I'll help you to finally enjoy promoting what you do.

Ready to go? Let's start where it all began.

The Best 90 Days Ever

The Best 90 Days Ever first came about after a launch that didn't quite go to plan.

A few summers ago, a friend and I created a course to help business owners with their marketing and mindset. We planned a great launch, we ran a free challenge and we did all the posts, videos and podcasts that I would recommend to anyone else. But no one signed up.

I would never say a launch is a failure because launching has so many benefits to your business. We were more visible and grew our email lists, we created some great content, people learnt useful information, but of course it was disappointing that no one joined us.

If I'm being really honest, I'd planned for that money to come into the business and when it didn't, I was stuck. It was the middle of September and I had no idea what I was going to do over the next few months to bring in more income before Christmas.

I spoke to my dad on the phone and he said, 'Give me at least three ideas of what you're going to do before the weekend, and then you're going to pick one'. I grabbed my giant whiteboard and some pens and sat down in the living room to think about what I was going to do.

A few ideas came to mind at first. A Christmas workshop and one-to-one sessions, or going out and getting more social media management work, but the thing I couldn't get out of my head was a daily task to help you promote your business.

I'd been doing a course that gave you a journaling prompt each day and I thought 'I wonder what that would look like if it helped you with your marketing instead?'

By then it was almost October and there were 3 months left of the year, just over 90 days. I felt like I was stuck with what to do and on a dog walk with Tom I asked, 'What would it take to make these next few months the best few months ever?' That doesn't quite have the same ring to it, so I did some research on the ideal amount of time to focus on your goals and 90 days kept coming up, the same amount roughly as each quarter of the year.

The Best 90 Days Ever had a good ring to it, so I told my dad the idea and decided to get to work on it. **Coming up with 90 different 10-minute tasks isn't easy.** But I had a hair appointment that week where I would be sitting in the same chair for a few hours so I told myself if I could write 30 of the 90 daily prompts then I would go for it. Fifty-six prompts later and I knew I was on to something.

I had only planned to run it for that 90 days but after the first launch of The Best 90 Days Ever I realized this could be the marketing membership that I'd really wanted for my business. Here we are with a daily marketing prompt in the group over 2 years later!

In The Best 90 Days Ever we have weekly themes with a daily marketing prompt, co-working sessions on Zoom, our 'A Morning of Marketing' batch creating workshop, coaching sessions and fun challenges like 'Back to Business Bootcamp'.

We now have over 50 different themed weeks, and I create new themed weeks for every launch we do.

Hundreds of small business owners have been a part of the group and they say time and time again that it is such a supportive community to be in.

This book is based on The Best 90 Days Ever daily marketing membership and 13 of our favourite weekly themes. There's plenty more where these came from if you'd like to come and join us.

I really hope you enjoy reading this as much as I have enjoyed writing these prompts and running this group. Sometimes things don't go the way we hoped they would, but another idea is right around the corner.

Why 10-minute marketing works

I wish I could say that there is a scientific reason why this book is based on 10-minute marketing prompts, but the reality is that it's just roughly how long it takes to make a good cup of tea.

Ten-minute marketing has really changed how my business works. I am someone who gets very distracted. Long periods of focused work are quite difficult and not something I can consistently do every day, especially for my own business. I enjoy talking about what I do, so I needed to find a way to make that a part of my working routine.

We often overestimate how long things are going to take us, especially jobs we don't want to do. I watched a video on TikTok where someone said that the way she convinces herself to do a chore is by looking at the clock, doing the task (like putting something away) and looking at the clock again to see that the time hasn't changed and it took less than a minute to do.

We are all busy and one of the things I hear the most often from other business owners is 'I just don't have time'. I get it, between your business, other work commitments, family and friends there doesn't feel like there are spare hours to commit to writing a post to share on Instagram. But maybe you could find 10 minutes instead?

In our minds marketing is a big task, but you can get results in a small amount of time.

I'm realistic that 10 minutes is not a life changing amount of time to spend on your business. Chances are you won't completely write a blog post or record and edit a podcast in that time.

But if you spend just 10 minutes working on your marketing over 90 days, that's an extra 15 hours over 3 months that you weren't spending before. If I asked you to find 15 hours of 'spare' time I'm sure you would be just as horrified as I was.

Ten minutes is enough to get the ball rolling, get projects started, get ideas out of your head and onto a sheet of paper or a Google doc where you can start making progress on them. It might not feel life changing at the time, but keep putting all those small actions together and you've made 90 positive changes to your business.

If you do read this book and think 'I can't even find 10 minutes today' that's okay. Give it 1 minute. Give it a thought while you're in the shower, walking the dog or sitting in traffic. Just thinking about your marketing can help you make progress too.

But if you do have extra time, make the most of it. Circle the tasks that you want to come back to and spend more time on, fold the pages down and make notes on it. This is your book to get creative with and enjoy.

How to have The Best 90 Days Ever

When it comes to having The Best 90 Days Ever, it's all about experimenting with what's going to get you the best results.

I know that I'm in a privileged position with my business where I can afford to try new things and not rely on them having a positive outcome. Not everyone is in the same position and for lots of businesses this might be their last chance to make things work.

We have lost so many innovative brands and spaces that support the community over the last few years and it can be tough out there if you're self-employed.

The Best 90 Days Ever is designed to fit in around the rest of your day, so as long as you can find 10 minutes to work on your marketing, you should be able to complete this book. I hope that means the risk is low as you can still work on the other parts of your business without taking time and energy away from them.

This book is designed to be a daily task to work through over a quarter of the year, but I know that not everyone works that way.

If you want to start on day 1 and work through a task each day for 90 days, you'll make progress quickly. But if you know you don't have much time and you'd like something that feels less structured you can also pick up this book any day and choose a task at random.

Why not use a random number generator and let it decide what you're going to work on?

You can work through these prompts as many times as you need to, and you'll find that you pick up different things each time. This book works for all stages of business, and it will help you with ideas at any point. There are members in the group who are just starting up and there are members who are much further on in their journey too.

The Best 90 Days Ever is designed to start on a Monday in any month of the year. Each week we have simple tasks on the weekend that are easier to fit in if you aren't planning to be at your laptop. That doesn't mean you have to wait for a Monday to begin, but you might find that some of the tasks aren't how you'd like to be spending your Sunday morning!

There are some topics that you won't find in this book, unfortunately I'm not able to cover everything about marketing in just 90 days. In particular, you might notice that I don't mention paid adverts (ads).

I think paid adverts have an important place in the marketing strategy for many small business owners, but so far, my marketing has been organic and I don't have experience with ads. If this is something you're interested in I would highly recommend finding an expert that can support you to build this into your plan. Mistakes can be costly and there are some fantastic businesses that specialize in helping you get the most from your ad investment.

You'll find some extra resources on my website including a 90-day habit tracker, so you can mark off the completed tasks as we go: www.hicommunications.co.uk/thebest90dayseverbook

 There's also a printable workbook with space and ideas to help you with some of the tasks in this book so you can make notes as you think of them. When you spot the pencil icon at the end of the task, this means there is a

page in the workbook for you to complete. I hope this book sparks lots of ideas for you and the workbook gives you a space to store them.

If you're ready, let's get started and have 'the best 90 days ever'!

Month 1

Week 1: Goal setting and planning your goals for the next 90 days

Welcome to *The Best 90 Days Ever*! I'm really excited to get started and work together for the next 3 months.

The Best 90 Days Ever always starts in the same way with goal setting week. This is the best way to get results out of the next 3 months because you have a clear direction and an aim that you're working towards.

If you don't know where you're heading, how will you know if you've made progress? Setting goals means you can check in along the way, see how brilliantly you're doing and keep motivated to continue putting in the hard work to improve your marketing.

In the first week you're going to set your goals and break them down into small, achievable chunks that you can work towards.

I would recommend doing these tasks at the start of every quarter if you can. Even putting an hour aside every few months will help you to notice which of your goals you're procrastinating on and where you've made the most progress.

Day 1: Re-introduce yourself on social media

For our first task we always introduce ourselves and focus on bringing the group together in the online membership, but as you're working through this as a book you're going to do something different.

Today's task is to re-introduce yourself on a social media platform of your choice. You could go live on Instagram, create a graphic for LinkedIn, record a video for TikTok or even write a blog post for your website that gives us more information. Tell us what you do, why you started and you can even share what your goals are for the next 90 days.

I'll break the ice. I'm Hannah, I live in Barry in South Wales with my partner, Tom, and our chocolate Labradors, Bernie and Lacey. I've been self-employed for a long time, mainly as a social media manager but I also have digital courses and run The Best 90 Days Ever marketing membership. Tom is a graphic designer and photographer, and we work together on lots of different projects. I love car boot sales, charity shops and our home is filled with wicker so if you ever spot a piece send it my way!

Are you ready to share yours?

You can include as many details as you want to with this task but make sure it's something you feel comfortable with. When there are lots of people in a similar industry to you, sharing parts of your personality like this can really help to set you apart from the rest.

If you're up for it, you can also make it into a fun challenge for your audience such as a post that includes 'two truths and a lie' or 'five facts about me that you didn't know'. Have some fun with this and start a conversation with your followers so they can find out more about you and you can find out more about them.

Good luck! I'm really excited to see all your posts, if you'd like to tag me so I can cheer you on you can find me at @hicommunications_

Day 2: Pick your word or theme for the next 90 days

Today's task is to pick your word or theme for the next 90 days. This is a great task for January if you don't feel like setting resolutions, but it's also a good idea to do it throughout the year to help you create checkpoints and check in on how you're doing.

We used to do this task at the start of the year in the membership, but I realized that this is a great way to guide how you want to feel each quarter, so we include it in every round of The Best 90 Days Ever now.

When you're setting goals or making plans for the month you can think about whether they fit with the word you've decided for that quarter. If they don't, is there a way to adapt them so that they do? Or maybe it's a sign to move some of your plans to a different part of the year where they would be a better fit.

If you've picked 'rest' for the next 3 months, it's probably not the best time to plan a monthly launch. If you've picked 'growth' then it's time to get out of your comfort zone and that might take some energy.

My word of the year has been things like determined, momentum or consistent. As I'm writing this my word for this year is 'bold'. What will yours be?

Here are a few suggestions but feel free to take a look online for some others if you need inspiration, there are some great word-of-the-year blog posts on Pinterest.

Consistency. Thrive. Creativity. Compassion. Courage. Brave. Collaborate. Action. Rest. Balance. Engage. Fearless. Growth. Change. Simplify. Community. Strength. Freedom. Love. Health. Yes. No. Grateful. Committed. Pause. Movement. Lead. Routine. Imagination.

Do any of these stand out to you? Get your word written down somewhere you can see it and keep coming back to it.

Remember this is your word and it has to feel right for you. If you pick a word but it doesn't quite fit the feeling of what you're going for this quarter, change it. This word has to fit how you feel and we can't always predict the opportunities and possibilities that are going to come our way.

 Write your word of the quarter in your workbook so you can see it every time you work on your business.

Day 3: Set yourself three goals

If you want to make a change over the next 90 days, the best way is to set yourself achievable goals to focus on for the future.

These 90 days are for you and your personal and business goals. Everyone's aims will be different and that's what makes this so exciting. You'll also find your goals are likely to change each time you read this book or even as you are completing the tasks and getting clearer on your business vision.

Today's task is to decide three goals for the next 90 days.

The way you set your goals is up to you. Some of us like to create three overall goals to work on over the 90 days and others like to set one goal for each month. If you think you might feel overwhelmed working on all three goals then try and break them down into monthly goals that reflect what you have coming up in your business.

Think about these three questions to help you create three main goals you would like to achieve over the next 90 days.

1. What tasks have been on your to-do list?
2. Where do you want to focus your attention for the next 90 days?
3. Is there a part of your business that you want to work on?

If you're struggling with these questions here are a few of the goals I've seen from previous members of The Best 90 Days Ever.

o Finally start an email newsletter
o Get three new coaching clients
o Create a working routine
o Be consistent on social media
o Refresh my current website

Our goals are all different and just like the word you're choosing for these 3 months, if you feel like your goals have changed then don't be afraid to swap them out for new ones.

I would recommend storing these goals somewhere that you can see them regularly like your workbook. I have mine in my Trello board, which is an online project management tool, and for our membership group we create a big document of goals that we can check in on. I really like using Trello because you can add your information to the board in 'cards' and these can be moved around. You can label the cards, give them dates and it's a very visual tool which makes it great for tasks like goal setting or creating content.

You might like to share these goals or what's coming up for you in a social media post. This is a great way to talk to your audience about what's happening so they know what to expect from you for the rest of the year. It might also give you that extra push to commit to making it happen.

A post that says 'here's what's coming up in the next few months' lets your audience know the best ways to work with you or buy from you and helps to bring them along for the ride!

 Add your three goals to your workbook and see how you feel about them once they're written down.

Day 4: Decide ten action steps for each one

Now that you have planned out your three main goals for the next 3 months, I want to help you create a strategy so you can actually achieve them.

Your task for today is to take your three 90-day goals and come up with ten of the smallest, simplest action steps for each one.

As you're doing this, notice how you feel about each step. If you've added a step to your list that you know you'll look at and feel overwhelmed by or tempted to procrastinate on, see if you can find an even smaller step first.

Many people don't achieve their goals because they feel like they are too big and out of reach. They are focusing on the end goal, rather than thinking about how they are going to get there and what they need to do each day. For example, 'get to 10,000 Instagram followers' feels huge when you first create your account, but 'come up with ten post ideas' is much smaller and easier to achieve.

When you're setting goals it's good to aim big, but when you're picking your action steps, you want to aim as small as possible.

Our action steps are the stepping stones to help us achieve our goals. We should look at them and know that they are something doable we could work on each day.

As you're ticking off your action steps you'll feel like you are moving closer towards your goal which really helps with motivation and keeps you moving forward.

Here's an example of ten action steps for the goal of 'starting an email newsletter':

1. Research three email platforms and sign up for a free trial
2. Play around with each one and see which feels like a good fit
3. Create an account on my chosen platform
4. Explore the templates that are already there for me to use
5. Make notes on what my first email will be about
6. Look at other email newsletters for inspiration (but don't copy!)
7. Create a landing page or simple way for people to sign up
8. Share my landing page and start getting subscribers

9. Write my first email in a Google doc
10. Put my email in the template and send it

Each of these smaller steps feels much more achievable than just 'start an email newsletter' and you'll find you're more likely to get on with it and get them done.

Online member, Lucy Price, who runs Lucy Hannah Photography, said, 'I always love the goal setting week. I find it really intimidating trying to plan out a whole year, or things change and it feel like you've failed those bigger goals. Whereas setting them every 90 days makes things feel much more achievable. You can look at the bigger picture but still be flexible as things change throughout the year. It definitely helps me stick to goals better and actually do the things to achieve them.'

As you're working through these steps over the next 3 months don't be afraid to add in a few more if the next task in front of you feels overwhelming. These are your goals and you have to find the best way of achieving them that works for you. Good luck on your steps!

 Write ten small action steps underneath each of your three goals and try to put them in a logical order of how you would complete them.

Day 5: Send yourself a letter to the future

Do you ever wish that you could talk to your future self and let them know that they're doing a great job and just need to keep going? This task will help you do just that.

Today's task is to schedule an email or use a website like www. futureme.org to send a message to yourself in the future. If you visit the FutureMe website you can read other public but anonymous letters and it's really interesting to see that most of them have a similar theme about getting through tough times.

If you're struggling with your business right now, send a letter to your future self to let them know that things are going to get better. You could send them an email with what you hope your ideal day at work would look like or what your big goals and visions are for your business.

You can do this task at the beginning of the year and send it to be opened at the end of December, or you could also send the email to be received at the end of these 90 days. Why not do both!

Once you start typing it gets much easier to talk to your future self, but here are some prompts to get you started. I would write these in a separate document first so you could add to them over the course of the day.

o How you feel now and how you hope to feel at the end of the 90 days
o Your goals and what you're aiming to achieve in the next 3 months
o Some things you want to start doing or hope you've stopped doing
o Any personal goals or events coming up and how you hope they'll go
o Your big picture vision for your life and business
o Words of motivation or something that will make future you happy

When you've written out your notes, pop them in an email and choose a date in 3 months' time to receive it.

I really loved receiving my emails and it's something I am going to do every 90 days now. It's so interesting to see how much can change in just 3 months.

If you enjoy this task, why not try sending a letter even further into the future too?

Day 6: Look at your strong and weak areas

This task is designed to help you dig a little deeper to find out what's working and more importantly, what isn't working for your marketing at the moment.

Looking at your analytics on social media and on your website is a really useful way to check in and find out more about your business so we can see what we need to do more of, and importantly what to do less of in the next quarter. Your analytics are the data from those platforms that shows features including views, reach, comments, likes and more.

Add 'check your analytics' to your routine so you always feel on top of the numbers in your business. Take a look at the data on Instagram, your email newsletter opens, your website page statistics, anything that can give you a better idea of what's working and what isn't.

Here are some questions to answer. You could write these down in your workbook, journal or add them to a project management tool like Trello or a Notion page to look at each month.

o   Which is your strongest area?
o   Which is your weakest area?
o   What brings in the most sales, messages or enquiries?
o   Where would you like to be more consistent?
o   Where do you want to focus your energy over the next 3 months?

Be honest with your answers, these are just for you and you don't need to share them. When you've finished this task, compare your answers to what your goals are for this quarter.

If email marketing brings in the most sales but it's your weakest area, you might want this to be a bigger focus in your business.

If TikTok doesn't bring in much engagement or enquiries but you've added it as one of your goals, is this the best place to use your time and energy? Only you will be able to tell.

The more information you have, the easier it is to make decisions about where to focus your time going forward.

 Think about your strongest and weakest areas and write them down in your workbook.

Day 7: Decide how you're going to track your goals

Today's task is to decide how you are going to track your goals, progress and stay organized. Goals are much harder to achieve when we set them, write them in a notebook and never look at them again. For these 3 months add them somewhere you know you'll be reminded of them to help you stay on track. You could use your workbook for this, or you might also find a digital tool works well so you can access it on the go.

In our membership group we add all of our goals and action steps to a Google Doc or Miro board which is a website full of online sticky notes. Some of our members also like to print off their goals and action steps so they can see them every day.

Here are some of the tools you could use.

o You might want to start a new notebook that is just for *The Best 90 Days Ever*. Make sure this is a notebook you use often or every day, the goals still need to be visible to you.

o Use an electronic method or a website like Trello, Asana or Notion. I personally love Trello and will mention it often in this book, but it isn't for everyone so find the option that works the best and you are most likely to use.

o If you want to get creative you could make a vision board. I love doing this for each season. My summer vision board might have the beach and an Aperol Spritz, but my winter vision board is all about getting cosy and working on some of the projects I've been putting off. Why not create a business vision board with your main goals?

I would encourage you to experiment with this task and see what works for you. I have used all three of these at different points and as I write this I have my vision board in the background of my laptop reminding me what my goals are for this round of *The Best 90 Days Ever*.

Remember you can change this at any time. If you start a Notion board and it doesn't click, move on to something else. These are your goals to track and achieve in the way that works best for you.

You can also use this task to think about milestones or ways you will know if you've achieved your goal.

This doesn't have to mean X number of followers or a huge increase in email subscribers, it could be just the way you feel about a part of your business. The choice is up to you, but I would definitely recommend a little reward when you've reached it.

Week 1: Checklist

Well done, you've completed the first week of *The Best 90 Days Ever*! How do you feel?

These goals will help to guide you over the next few months and get you closer to what you want your business to look like. If you feel yourself losing focus and drifting away from your goals, set aside some time to come back to them again. It might mean the goals need tweaking or your action steps could be adjusted. Make this work for you.

Tick these tasks off once you've completed them and if there are any you need to come back to, put a date in your diary to finish them.

☐ Re-introduce yourself on social media
☐ Pick your word or theme for the next 90 days
☐ Set yourself three goals

☐ Decide ten action steps for each one
☐ Send yourself a letter in the future
☐ Look at your strong and weak areas
☐ Decide how you're going to track your goals

Week 2: Batch creating content – How to have a bank of content ready to share

Welcome to batch creating week!

Over the next 3 months of *The Best 90 Days Ever* we're going to work on some marketing tools that you might not have looked at or focused on before. It's very exciting, but if you're like me and get distracted by shiny objects you might also find it hard to focus.

This week is all about batch creating a big bank of content for you to use over the next 90 days to make sure that even when you're testing out new templates or exploring how PR could work for your business, you'll still have a steady stream of consistent posts to share.

Consistency is really important for marketing. That doesn't mean posting every second of every day, but it does mean deciding what consistency looks like for you at different times of the year and sticking to it.

Batch creating content means working on the same type of content during a period of time to get it done quicker, better and more effectively.

It could be video content, grid posts, a series of emails or anything that you could create multiple pieces of to use in your marketing. It's a great tool to help you cut down the time you're spending on your phone and also get better results as you're able to dedicate a chunk of time to finding your flow and doing your best work. This helps to make consistency so much easier.

I haven't even mentioned how great it feels knowing you have a huge Trello board full of posts ready to go. Shall we get started and get batching together?

Day 8: Start a big content mind map

Our first task for this week is one I like to do in every round of The Best 90 Days Ever and most of the workshops I run. You're going to make a mind map.

When you're batch creating content the worst thing you can do is start with a blank screen on your laptop. Even when I began writing this book I used some of the prompts we have previously shared in the group.

To avoid the dread of the blank screen, I always like to have some notes to work from and this task is going to help with that.

Before you begin, you'll need a big piece of paper or you can use the template in your workbook, lots of coloured pens and a timer for 10 minutes.

Set the clock and challenge yourself to write down EVERYTHING you could talk about relating to your business. Words, themes, phrases, problems, solutions, things your customers have said and ideas. Put it all down!

Start with a big theme and keep going until you have lots of smaller themes. The example I like to use for this is one of our members Jon Evans who is a running coach at Jon Evans Coaching.

In the middle of Jon's mind map would be 'running', that's the main theme and the link between all of the content. Coming off of those branches could be long distance, short distance, nutrition, training plans, shoes, strength training, marathons and parkruns.

For each of those branches you can look even closer at things like protein and carbs, gait analysis, the pros and cons of each marathon or parkrun, which exercises to do and which to avoid. If you really want to you could get even more specific.

Do you see how as you look at each topic closely, more content ideas appear? Keep going with this for 10 minutes and see what comes up for you.

Now the trick for this task is to keep your piece of paper out where you can see it for the next 90 days. Keep adding to it as you think of ideas, I can almost guarantee you'll think of one in the shower! When you want to sit down and write a post, you'll have all of these prompts to get you started.

I'd recommend starting to add these into your Trello board or the platform you have decided as your digital storage solution.

 Use the template in your workbook to create your own content mind map.

Day 9: Try using content pillars

When was the last time you felt like you had a plan for your content? Most of the time we think we need to spend hours scheduling content when what we really need is a plan that keeps us on track and reminds us of the type of content we haven't posted recently.

If you're struggling to feel organized, one thing that works well for me is having 'content pillars'. These are themes of content that help to narrow down the type of posts you could share and group them into categories.

I don't like these to be too rigid, but I've found they really help me to treat batch creating content as more of a 'drag and drop' exercise. If I know the content I need to tick off and I can see themes I haven't posted about recently, I can sit and write that type of post and drop it into each of my content pillars.

Here are two options to help you set out your week. This is a reminder that you should only use these if they work for **you**. You might want to take little bits and adapt them or create your own content pillars. As always just take what you need and leave the rest.

Content pillar 1 – types of content:

1. **Selling/promotional** – What can people buy from you this week?
2. **Educational** – How can you educate them on a topic?
3. **Shareable** – What would they want to share on their social media?
4. **Personal** – A post about you or your brand
5. **Entertaining** – A meme or reel to make them laugh
6. **User-generated content** – Pictures, reviews, testimonials

Content pillar 2 – themed day plan:

Day 1 – What you're working on this week
Day 2 – Themed reel with an original audio or voiceover
Day 3 – Who, what, where, when, why post
Day 4 – Review or testimonial
Day 5 – General reel with trending audio

The reason these pillars work well is because not only do they give you inspiration for what to write, they also remind you of the content you haven't shared in a while. Every time I see this task I remind myself that I haven't shared a testimonial or review!

Your task for today is to map out a rough idea of what a great week of content would look like for you. Make it easy for you to follow, but also include the types of posts you know you've been avoiding because you find them challenging.

Save this plan somewhere you can keep coming back to it.

 Plan your weekly content pillars with examples of the types of post you could use.

Day 10: Batch create content for 30 minutes

Now that you have some ideas and a rough plan for your week, it's time to start batch creating!

Your task for today is to set a timer in 10-minute blocks, put your phone away and start writing as many post ideas as you can using those words you wrote on your mind map.

These posts don't need to be perfect, you aren't going to schedule or share them right away. The aim of this task is simply to get you into the flow of writing.

I know this can feel quite daunting but it's really important to put perfection to one side and just get into the habit of writing out ideas. Give yourself a reward at the end of this, a cup of tea usually works for me!

Online member, Hannah Lowe, works for The Cariad Blanket Project which supports women with free care and craft packages. She has been using the batch creating tasks to get her content prepared and ready. She said:

> *The batch creating tasks really helped me to get my content pre-made, where I had felt a mental block before in creating content. Having posts batch created meant I felt able to show up consistently on social media, and this led to more requests for the free care packages the charity sends out, smashing the target set by the trustees for the year.*

We were very lucky to be able to have Hannah at one of our in-person workshops just before her son made his appearance into the world!

As a bonus task see if you can schedule a 30-minute block each day this week. It might mean getting up 30 minutes earlier or moving some things around, but if you can make time for small chunks of focused writing you will really get ahead with your content.

When you've done this task make sure you add these posts into the place where you store your content. I use Trello for mine because it has an app that I can use on my phone but there are many different tools and schedulers to try. Do this as you go along or after your 30-minute session so you don't lose all these brilliant words you've started writing.

Day 11: Ask your audience questions

When we're creating content we will often think about the posts that we *think* our audience wants to see, rather than what they *tell* us they want to see.

Just like on *Who Wants to Be a Millionaire?*, you can also 'ask the audience' questions and see the answers you receive. They can spark ideas for things like posts, blogs and newsletters and also show you what type of content to share more and less of.

Today your task is to pick a platform and get to know your audience by asking them some specific questions. For this task the phrase 'What do you want to see from me?' is banned!

My two favourite ways to do this are with surveys and on Instagram stories, but you can do this in your emails, on Facebook and LinkedIn or most other platforms.

Surveys

Surveys are a great tool to find out more about how your audience is feeling, what they're struggling with and what they need help or support with. They are good for getting longer answers when you want people to feel that it's a safe and private space to share.

The positives are that you often get more detailed responses and people will share more in a survey if you ask the right questions. The negatives are that it can be a big ask to get people to give up their time to answer your questions so some might need an incentive like a discount code or entry into a competition. You also need to spend some time on your questions if you want to get the right answers that will help you with your content or creating new offers based on what they've said.

Stories

The other option is Instagram stories which have a variety of poll features on their story stickers, just look for the smiley face in the box at the top when creating your story. You can do a question box, a slider, polls or quizzes and give your audience options like 'what's your biggest struggle?', 'What would you like to improve?', 'Do you want to see more of X or more of Y?'

The positives with Instagram are that it's a quick return. It's easy to put up your questions and easy for your audience to answer them as they are flicking through. If you know the questions and they have a very specific answer, stories can be useful. For example, if you ask questions like 'do you like the red mug or the blue mug?' you're going to get some good feedback.

The negatives are that if you have a smaller or less engaged audience you might not get many responses. Keep trying and tweak the questions slightly to make them even easier and enjoyable to answer.

You might also find your replies are limited to the options you are able to give. The question box is small and unless people send you a private message you could be looking at just a few sentences for each person.

Stories polls are still worth doing and great for engagement. I love to do polls to figure out the general feeling of my community and see how everyone is doing in each season.

When you get your information back, make sure to look at what your ideal clients have said. Sometimes we will get feedback that isn't relevant for us because they aren't our ideal client and weren't planning to buy anyway. You also don't want to assume that everyone who replies to your story is going to buy your product or service. This isn't an accurate way to decide the demand.

Look at the feedback from your survey and quizzes and see how many posts you can create from them. You could do general educational posts or even use the answers to create a blog featuring members of your community, with their permission of course. Use the platform that makes the most sense for you.

Give yourself 10 minutes, pick the platform you are using the most to talk to your audience and adapt the questions to suit the features you have to work with.

Day 12: Reuse big and small pieces of content

Today I'm going to teach you my favourite way to batch create and a trick if you want people to say 'wow how do you have time to create so much content?'

Today's task is about reusing content, taking something that you've already written and turning it into a different post that you can use. There are two ways that you can do this and they can potentially just take 10 minutes, but you might also want to spend longer on it.

The first way is by taking a bigger piece of content like a blog or newsletter and turning it into lots of smaller pieces of content. This could be something you've previously written and still feels relevant and true for your business that you can use again in a smaller format like a grid post or a story.

But you can also do this in reverse and gather up some of your smaller pieces of content to make a bigger article. On day 11 we spoke about using some of the answers from your survey to create a blog post, that would be a great example of this!

One of the easiest ways of doing this and explaining how it works is by using a numbered list post. For example…

Five ways…
Five lessons…
Five things…
Five shifts…
Five habits…
Five steps…
Five products…
Five hacks…
Five lifestyle changes…

I've used the number five as an example for this, but you could use any amount, I've seen blog posts that go up to as many as 100.

Pick one of these and look through some of your previous posts to see if you've shared any individual tips that you can gather together. They can be quite short and snappy, we are just getting the ball rolling for this task.

When you've created a shorter post, see if you can add some more information to each 'tip' to make it the right length to be longer, like a blog post.

When you've done that, challenge yourself to look through your content and get as many ideas as you can for..:

o   A blog
o   A newsletter
o   A post
o   A topic for a live
o   An idea for a reel
o   An Instagram story

You've written lots of content that can be reused, it's just about finding it.

Today's task is to decide whether to take something bigger and make it smaller, or to take smaller pieces and make them into a bigger piece of content. Decide what you want to do and see how much you can squeeze the juice out of that content.

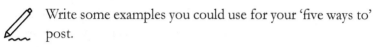 Write some examples you could use for your 'five ways to' post.

Day 13: Look at the images and videos you can reuse

Hopefully by this point you've managed to write lots of words that you can use in your marketing and you can see where more content can be easily found. But what about the images to go with them?

I am very lucky that my partner (and husband by the time this book comes out!), Tom, is a graphic designer and a photographer so he is always on hand to help with photos and the way my graphics look. He has definitely taught me a lot about how important consistency is and how to bring more of that into my marketing visuals. But what if you don't have a photographer/graphic designer husband? Don't worry, you have options.

This is something that I would definitely recommend outsourcing if you have the budget for it. Professional headshots look exactly that – professional, and you can use them in lots of different places including your website, blog, emails and social media.

If you're a product business, one of our members, Lucy, that I mentioned earlier in goal setting week, has an affordable monthly content subscription where you send over your products and each month you'll receive photos and videos back. Genius!

You can also outsource your social media graphics or buy a set of templates that you can customize with your own brand colours.

But if you're not quite at that place, and because I still need to give you a 10-minute task, here's another way around it.

Today's task is to see how many photos and videos you already have available to use that go with all the brilliant content you've written this week. Let's go on a treasure hunt and see what we can find.

Start with the photos on your phone. Are there photos here that you could use for a post? I love sharing a photo dump of some of my favourite pictures from that month. This is great for seasonal photos too, try searching the month we're in on your phone's photo album and seeing if you have any images from previous years that you could use again.

What about videos? Short snippets of video can make quick and easy reels or you can film yourself answering questions or explaining topics.

Could you snap a picture or set up a video of your coffee this morning? If you move your laptop near the window, is the lighting better?

Maybe you have previously had a photoshoot and it's worth taking a second look through the photos to see which ones you could use again or if you missed any. Photos don't have to be professionally taken every time, but if you do have professional photos make sure you're making the most of them.

If you can't find any, could you spend an hour today taking some images? Look for inspiration on Pinterest or Instagram and see if you can find photographers that offer great phone photography tips.

Plan different events for next week that could give you good opportunities for photos, like a coworking space, coffee shop or workshop.

If in doubt, some natural light, a tidy office and a cup of tea is a good place to start. Get your phone out and start snapping!

Day 14: Plan out the number of posts you need to create

The final step for batch creating week is going to set you up for success for the rest of these 90 days. It's all about planning. When I think about marketing my business, sometimes it feels like a huge task that will never really be done. But honestly? That is partly right. There is always something to do.

I find it much easier to think about the year in seasons and luckily that works out at roughly every 90 days. Instead of thinking about the year as a whole, think about your marketing in terms of the season or quarter in front of you. It's much easier to plan for and can stop that overwhelm from creeping in.

In an ideal world we'd all have huge teams that can plan campaigns years in advance and have a big budget to spend, but most of us are small business owners working on our own, outsourcing things when we can.

To make your marketing easier, your final task is to look ahead at the next few months and think about it in numbers. Decide how many posts you need to create, how many newsletters you'd like to send or blog posts you want to write.

When I'm doing this for a season I like to set a minimum amount and a maximum target goal for how much I could create if I'm feeling good.

For example, over the summer months my minimum will be lower than during winter, because I don't plan to be at my laptop as much. But when I'm in a launch period promoting the next round of The Best 90 Days Ever my minimum content is much higher because I want to be visible and I've planned it in advance.

Break your content down into something like this – for the next 3 months my minimum and maximum amount each month will be:

o   Minimum two newsletters, maximum four newsletters
o   Minimum two podcasts, maximum four podcasts
o   Minimum four reels, maximum 12 reels
o   Minimum 10 grid posts, maximum 30 grid posts

I know I keep repeating myself but adapt this if you need to. If your energy changes, so should your marketing plan.

This book is designed to make marketing easier, not more challenging.

 Write down how much content you need to create this season.

Week 2: Checklist

We made it to the end of our batch creating week! How have you found it?

I hope these prompts have shown you that planning in advance can end up saving you lots of time in the long run and reusing content is a good routine to get into. We want to be repetitive in our messaging and remember, only a small number of people see everything you post.

Most will only catch snippets here and there so if they remember what you posted last year I'd be very surprised.

Tick off these tasks as you complete them and add in some batch creating time to your calendar for the next few months.

☐   Start a big content mind map
☐   Try using content pillars
☐   Batch create content for 30 minutes
☐   Ask your audience questions
☐   Reuse big and small pieces of content
☐   Look at the images and video you can reuse
☐   Plan out the number of posts you need to create

Week 3: PR – Using PR to grow your business

Before I started my business, HI Communications, and decided I wanted to be self-employed, my background was in social media and PR. I worked for a charity and then a housing association and some exciting things happened while I was there, but I still feel like I'm learning more about PR as I go, especially when it comes to small businesses.

PR means Public Relations and I see it as the things you can do to increase your visibility and help more people find out about you and your brand. I've been on both sides of the coin for this, as a business owner looking for good PR opportunities and as a publication when we were running our digital magazine, Barry Magazine. I've definitely seen some interesting press releases end up in our inbox.

PR comes in lots of shapes and sizes. It could be being featured in a magazine, or it could be a guest on a podcast.

You're probably already doing more PR than you think, but if it is a focus for you, I would highly recommend looking at someone who can help you. Many PR professionals offer one-to-one sessions that will give you plenty of ideas and strategies to work on.

I'd also suggest reading the book *Hype Yourself* by Lucy Werner which is also published by Practical Inspiration Publishing for lots of brilliant PR advice.

But while you're here, I've got seven 10-minute tasks for you to give you a taste of what PR can do and how you can get some quick wins to boost your business.

Day 15: Write a list of what makes you different

If you shy away from talking about yourself, I'm just going to warn you, you might find this week's tasks challenging. But if you can push through and get past the discomfort, they will be game-changing for your business.

When you're a small business owner there are bound to be lots of people that offer similar products or services as you. It can be frustrating and feel difficult to stand out from the crowd, but the thing I want you to remember is that what makes you different, is you.

Someone might have a similar service to you but had a varied journey to get there. They might sell the same products, but the story behind them is different. If you can get comfortable sharing what makes you unique and adding in some of that brilliant personality, you'll set yourself apart from others.

Today's task will hopefully get you started. Set your timer for 10 minutes and write a list of all the things that you are known for, things that make you or your business different or that you have an opinion about. You might not think you have a story, but you do, you just have to find it!

Some of the things I put on my own list are:

o I moved 200 miles from Bedfordshire to Barry and only knew one person there
o I decided to start my business mainly because I have Crohn's disease
o I have two rescue chocolate Labradors
o I love car boot sales, charity shops and finding a bargain! My house was featured in a magazine because I renovated it on a budget, we found my roll top bath on the side of the road and lots of the furniture was from skips
o I ran my first marathon for Crohn's and Colitis UK in 2021

Sometimes we get a PR opportunity for something that isn't directly related to our business but we can still mention our website in the article.

I was featured in *Fabulous* online and had a double page spread in *Women's Own* all about doing up my house for free, and although it wasn't related to marketing, it definitely increased traffic to my social media and website. My grandad still keeps a copy of the magazine in his living room!

Start your list today and keep adding to it as you think of things throughout this week. You could even ask friends and family for suggestions or encourage them to start their own list.

 Write down a list of what makes you and your business different.

Day 16: Go on X (formerly Twitter) and look at #JournoRequest

This is one of my favourite tasks of these 90 days because our members have had some amazing results from this and it truly is a 10-minute task.

Today's task is to look on X (formerly Twitter) at #JournoRequest to see if there are any relevant stories you can contribute to.

On #JournoRequest people who are writing articles and looking for input or someone they can feature will often put a call out that you can reply to. You might spot something and think, 'That's me!'

I just had a quick look and there are requests for health and fitness experts, travel destinations, HR managers, doctors, small business owners, retail experts, coaches and even specific events for Bristol. It varies every day and you'll be surprised by the opportunities that come up.

Remember our task from yesterday, this doesn't have to be specific to your business. There are plenty of things you can comment on that will help to get you and your brand more exposure. As you're reading through the requests from journalists, think about your list of personal features.

Louise Worrall who is a member of our online membership and runs 'Voyage of Hope Therapy Services' spotted a #JournoRequest and responded.

The finished article 'I'm a children's counsellor – the TV shows I let my kid watch and why In The Night Garden was banned in my household' was related to her industry and they also mentioned her business name and linked to her website which is great for SEO. She could then share the article for different posts, videos and even a blog post on her website too. That 10-minute task turned into multiple content opportunities and visibility for her business.

If PR is a focus for you, I would recommend adding this into your daily routine. It doesn't take long to have a quick look throughout the day and you could end up with some great free coverage.

The other thing I love about looking on #JournoRequest is finding opportunities for other people. In the group I will share the ones that I think could be relevant but I'll often message other business owners to say I saw this and thought of you.

It's a lovely way to share opportunities with other small business owners and everyone likes to know that someone is thinking of them!

Day 17: Get your PR folder organised and ready

Now that you've been doing the work to get noticed and looking for opportunities, you want to make sure you're ready for when they happen.

Press opportunities can have a very quick turnaround and if you're already writing something or preparing for an interview, the last thing you want is to waste time finding your headshots too.

Today's task is to get organized and be ready for when an opportunity comes your way. I was taught this in one of my first job roles and it makes sense for my business too.

In my work role I would have a folder with all the key information people would ask for. This was usually things like a logo in colour and black and white, general landscape and portrait photos that promoted the charity and a headshot of the person the article was talking about if it has someone specific. We also had some charity information and statistics on hand if we ever needed them quickly.

As a business owner, my folder also looks similar but it's more focused on me as a founder than the company as a whole. I have a range of headshots I can use that are ready to go, my basic biography which I can tweak slightly if I need to, my logo in different formats and my contact details.

If you are a product business, you might have product images for different seasons and if you own a shop you might have shop images to use too.

Sometimes getting a great piece of PR is about speed and being the fastest finger first, so be ready for when those opportunities come and have that folder on hand!

Day 18: Make a list of dream features

Today your task is to aim big and think about the dream places you would love to be featured. This could mean being interviewed on a podcast, writing a guest blog for a website, an interview in a newsletter, an article in a magazine, an expert opinion or even your own newspaper column.

Your aim this week is to show that you are an expert in your industry, so what can you do to get the word out there?

Set a timer for 10 minutes and write out a list of all the places you would love to get featured. Put down the big names, the little names and everything in between!

Don't overthink this, it's your list and these are your goals. If the opportunity does come up for a dream publication, it's up to you whether you say yes or no to it.

If you're struggling to think of anywhere, start by looking at some of the businesses who are slightly further along than you or you know have had some great press coverage.

Lots of businesses will have a section on their website saying 'featured in' or 'appeared on' and this is great for inspiration of places you would like to collaborate with.

You could also go into a shop that sells the type of magazines you would like to write for or take a look online to see if there are any digital editions you could contribute to.

Keep adding to this list and notice when you see another business get a piece of press coverage that you would love to feature in as well. I would also set this up in my Trello board so I can keep track of where I'd like to appear, where I've been featured and where others have featured too.

 Write a list of your dream features and aim high!

Day 19: Learn how to pitch in 6 steps

Today's task is all about *how* to pitch!

On day 18 you wrote out a list of places you would love to be featured and today you're going to start preparing a pitch to them.

This task can be applied to different media including podcasts, guest blogging and even magazine articles. Keep in mind the place or person you are pitching to and how you can adapt your pitch to each one.

This will take longer than 10 minutes, but some work upfront to get a draft of this will save you time in the long run!

1. Research where you're pitching to
   If it's a podcast, listen to it. If it's a blog, read it. If it's a magazine, buy a copy. Make sure you know what you're pitching to and why.

2. Who are you?
   Remember the bio you prepped the other day for your folder? Use this but shorter. Say who you are and why you are a good fit.

3. Do the work for them
   Suggest a topic in your pitch that relates to the place you're pitching. Try and be specific when you send this, I wouldn't be able to pitch to just talk about 'marketing' but 10-minute marketing for small businesses is much more specific. Look for gaps in what they have spoken about before and see where you fit in.

4. Use the research
   Mention that research you've done. If you loved a podcast episode tell them why, if you read a blog post, what was great about it?

5. Share examples
   If you don't have your own podcast, share some examples of when you've done some live videos or if you are pitching to write an article, share some of the articles you've previously written.

6. Keep it short!
   Don't make your pitch too long. The person you're pitching too will probably get lots of these so make sure you're keeping it quick and to the point.

If you want to break this down even more, try working on each of these elements for 10 minutes over the next few days and see how far you get. It's good to start putting yourself out there, whatever the answer to your pitch ends up being.

Day 20: Buy the magazines or listen to the podcasts

Okay I know I said that the #JournoRequest task was my favourite but I think this is possibly the best day ever and perfect for a weekend. If this task hasn't fallen on a weekend for you, it might be worth saving it for then or when you have a day off.

Your task for today is to go back to that list you made earlier of your dream publications and start to get really familiar with them.

Buy the magazines or newspapers of the places you want to be featured and spend some time reading them.

Make a note of what stories they include and the themes they are talking about. You could look at the names of the journalists and follow them on Twitter or LinkedIn to see if they share people they would like to speak to for future articles.

I would love to be featured in *Red* magazine one day and I have a monthly subscription to it so I can see the types of articles they publish throughout the year.

If you'd love to be part of your local paper, pick it up and start to see the types of stories they are sharing and how your story might link in too.

If one of your goals is to be featured on a podcast that you love, start listening to each of the episodes. Not only will you be able to mention the ones that you enjoyed the most when you pitch to them, you'll start to get a feel for their interview style and the questions they ask too.

Pop them a message on social media to let them know that you loved it and it might even start a relationship so that when you do get round to pitching, they already know who you are.

One of my old managers told me that a lot of PR is about relationships and that has been true for me, especially when it comes to social media and digital marketing.

If you have a good connection with someone over messages, chances are you're going to have a good connection for a podcast episode too!

Day 21: Join some PR groups and search for opportunities

This is your final task for PR week, and I wondered whether to include it because I want this book to give useful marketing advice that isn't going to date quickly, and I worry that this task will.

But as with all of the tasks in this book, you can take parts of them and adapt them to your own business or the current platforms you are using at the time.

Today's task is to join some PR groups that are relevant for your industry.

There are a few PR Facebook groups that I really like to use and every day new opportunities come up for stories, pitches and even work opportunities. One of my favourite groups is called *No.1 Freelance Media Women* which is really active and supportive.

There are plenty of free groups like this on Facebook and there are also paid membership groups that you can join and speak directly with the journalists.

As new social media platforms get popular, there will always be opportunities like this so see if you can scope out the best place to get the information from.

Week 3: Checklist

That brings us to the end of PR week! I hope that this week has shown you that those exciting PR opportunities you've secretly been dreaming of are possible for you.

Even small business owners can take steps to get some great PR for their business, and it can be done in just 10 minutes a day if you keep working on it. Have in mind the publications you want to connect with and go for it. What's the worst that could happen?

Here are your tasks to tick off when you've completed them!

- ☐ Write a list of what makes you different
- ☐ Go on Twitter and look at #JournoRequest
- ☐ Get your PR folder organized and ready
- ☐ Make a list of dream features
- ☐ Learn how to pitch in six steps
- ☐ Buy the magazines or listen to the podcasts
- ☐ Join some PR groups and search for opportunities

Week 4: Productivity – Learn the productivity tools to get stuff done

Now that we've started learning ways to promote our businesses, we also want to learn the tools to be more productive and get the work done.

One of the most common reasons I hear for businesses not working on their marketing is that they don't have time. But when these tasks are only taking 10 minutes, is that really the reason?

Everyone has a different capacity which can vary each day, but productivity is about making the most of the time you do have and using it in an effective way to help you get results. The aim of this week is less procrastinating, and more moving closer to those goals!

If you're ready to start getting the work done, read on.

Day 22: Find an accountability partner

This week we're going to look at ways to be more productive and the best place to start is with accountability.

Unfortunately, I can't be there to be a cheerleader for everyone who reads this book, but I bet you can find someone who will.

Today's task is to find yourself a partner you can check-in with for this week and beyond. You might want to choose a friend, colleague, family member or another business owner. It could be with our online membership or maybe you have found someone else who is reading this book at the same time as you!

Pick someone who you know will motivate you and help you to reach your goals. To make this successful, set up what you're expecting from the start. Do you want them to check in at the beginning of the day, or do you need someone watching you hourly?

Be realistic about how much support you need and how much someone will be able and willing to give you. If you're asking for advice, you might be looking for a coach instead.

I always turn to my friend Liz for accountability as she knows how to help me get stuff done. We message each other on WhatsApp and send voice notes when we have ideas.

I also do Voxer coaching with my one-to-one clients so they have someone that they can turn to and ask questions during the week. When you start moving forward in your business, often more hurdles will come up and you can feel stuck until you've worked through them.

I've always found that accountability is really important for productivity, whether it's with someone else or with goals I've set myself.

Decide what is going to work best for you this week and put a plan in place to make the most of the support to help you move forward.

Day 23: Notice when you're getting distracted

Remember those goals you set at the start? Don't lose sight of them. Ninety days is a great amount of time to make progress without forgetting the direction you're heading in, so go back and look at those goals today.

When you've got those goals in your mind, make a plan to minimize distractions this week so you can get the work done to move you forward.

If you're being honest, what distracts you each day? Is it your phone? Social media on your laptop? Emails pinging up? Someone else in your space? Knowing you have lots of other things to do? Throughout this week we're going to look at methods to stop some of these, but for today I want you to make a list of them and be aware of them each day.

I love working from home, but I know that there is a temptation to put the washing on or play with the dogs when I should be focusing. When I know I need to get work done I'll go to a co-working space, or when I planned to work on my eBook without distractions I booked a cheap airbnb in the next town to us and stayed there for a couple of nights so I could finish it.

I am very privileged to be able to do these things and be at a stage in my life where I can spend that time on my business, but there are still ways to bring some of these small moments into your everyday work too.

o It might be clearing your desk space so there are fewer distractions
o Setting up a meal plan for the week or having a basic work 'uniform' so you have fewer decisions to make
o Using the tools I'm going to mention on Day 24 to let technology help you and not get in the way
o Putting a limit on the amount of time you can procrastinate before you have to start work again

For today, notice where the distractions are and when they are derailing you from your work.

Day 24: The productivity tools that will help you

Today I want to share with you some of the productivity tools that I use to help me get work done.

Forest app

The number one for me is the Forest app, I couldn't do any focused work without this. www.forestapp.cc. The idea of Forest is that you set a time that you want to block your phone for and put it away. In that time it grows a tree to add to your forest, but if you pick the phone up during that time the tree will die.

They work with an organization to plant trees and it's strangely motivating knowing that if you pick up the phone it will kill the tree. For me it's an extra barrier to stop me mindlessly picking up my phone even if I've been hiding it in a drawer.

There is a small cost for this app, but there are plenty of similar tools you can use to block your phone and laptop too. I will usually have my laptop set to focus mode so that calls and sounds don't come through and distract me while I'm working. If you find yourself scrolling and procrastinating then look at some blocker apps you can use to keep you focused.

Habit trackers

I also like to use a habit tracking app on my phone where you can tick off what you've done each day and share the habits with your friend or accountability partner to keep you both on track.

If you search for a habit tracker there are plenty of apps to try, or you can even do this in your notebook or bullet journal too. You might find it useful to create your own tracker to print off, or take a look on Etsy to see the different designs available to save time.

Yellow timer

The other tool that I find really useful for productivity is my yellow timer. Setting a timer and working for that period of time has been so helpful and it's made me recognize those moments when I expect a task to take a long time but it is actually very quick.

It also helps with tasks that might feel big and overwhelming. If I can just get started and work on them for 10 minutes, I'm much more likely to keep going and make progress on those larger tasks that hang around on my to-do list.

The timer I use has a visual countdown so you can glance over and see how long you have left and it's perfect for jobs around the house too, not just work.

The timers have been a big hit for our online group, lots of the members have them and we use them to keep us focused.

These tools are all useful for productivity, but the trick is to keep them at the front of your mind so that when you get to work you don't forget to use them!

Go back to the list of distractions we wrote down and research a way that you can use a tool to reduce how much you procrastinate. There are so many useful methods out there, you just need to find a plan that works for you.

Day 25: Try The Pomodoro® Technique

If you need a method to help you be more productive with your time, you need to try the Pomodoro® Technique. The Pomodoro® Technique was developed by Francesco Cirillo in the late 1980s and is the method of time management that breaks your work into blocks to stop distractions.

To use the Pomodoro® Technique you start by deciding on your task and setting a timer for 25 minutes.

When that first block is finished you give yourself a 5-minute break and a chance to deal with some of the distractions that may have come up in that time. Go for a toilet break, make a cup of tea, get a snack and then get ready to come back to work.

When you're done you can start to work for another 25 minutes followed by a 5-minute break each time. If I have ideas or potential things that might be a distraction, I keep a notepad next to me so I can write them down and won't forget them. It means they are out of my head, but I can still come back to look at them later.

When you've completed four blocks of 25 minutes, give yourself a longer break of 15–20 minutes.

There is plenty of information online about the Pomodoro® Technique and even websites that will break down the tasks for you into easy blocks. It's great to help keep you focused and less distracted if you need something more structured for your working day.

This is one of the methods I've found that really works for me to help me focus on the task in front of me but there are plenty of other tools too.

Today's task is to explore some of the time management methods and give yourself space this week to test them out and see what works for you.

Day 26: Plan how long each of your tasks will take

When I started writing this book I gave myself a deadline that even I was surprised about. Not because I didn't think I could do it, but because I knew that the more time I gave myself, the longer it would take to get it done.

I've been reading about Parkinson's Law which is the idea that work fills the time that you give it. If I gave myself a year to write this book, it would take a year, but if I gave myself less time I would work to that deadline instead.

I use this with other work and call it the 'container strategy' which you might have seen some decluttering experts use too. The container strategy is where you limit what you have to fit into a certain container. For example, I use it for my socks, if they don't fit in that 'container' or drawer, it means some of them have got to go.

How does this link to productivity you might be asking? It's about putting limits on yourself to stop tasks and activities dragging on.

Today's task is to look at your to-do list and think about how long each task will take and how much time you are willing to give it. Instead of giving yourself a whole month to work on your next offer, could you spend 15 minutes planning the sales page or half a day editing the content?

Do you have a newsletter that you could write in 30 minutes if you set that time aside this week? Does a social media post really need to take an hour or would it be just as good if you set a limit of 10 minutes to get it done?

Make a note of how long you think each task will take and try to schedule it for next week. If you can make a note of how long each task *actually* took that's even better.

I find this quite eye opening because the tasks I'm procrastinating on will usually take less than an hour if I just get them done! You'll be surprised how quickly you can work through your tasks when you give them the right container.

Day 27: Try getting into a deep work zone

This task is all about 'deep work' which is a concept from Cal Newport. Deep work is when you are able to concentrate and get into a flow so you can get tasks done with focus or work on challenging tasks.

I have to be honest, I find this very difficult now when it comes to work. Outside of work if I'm gardening or crafting then I will hardly notice time has passed because I've been so focused on what I'm doing, but when I'm at work it feels different. We are distracted by social media, emails and notifications so it impacts our work and takes us longer to get back to focusing.

Today's task is to start to look at ways you can get into a deep work zone. I would recommend reading more on the topic too if it's something you are interested in! Here are some suggestions to get you started:

o Focus on one task at a time
o Decide the work that you're going to do before you start
o Block out chunks of time for deep work
o Put your phone in another room or use the Forest App to block distractions
o Stop emails flashing up while you're working and turn notifications off
o Let your colleagues or clients know when you are available
o Clear your desk and create space for focus

Deep work is one way to increase your productivity so try and see if you can schedule some time for deep work next week.

Day 28: Use the Eisenhower Matrix to plan your week

Today's task is to use your Sunday to plan the week ahead. With just a little bit of time set aside at the end of the weekend you can organize your time and it will really help with productivity. If it's not Sunday for you yet, plan this in for the end of the week! To do this you could look at a tool called the Eisenhower Matrix.

I make a big list of everything I have to do over the next week and keep it to hand so I can add to it. It's separate from my normal to-do list, but it means I don't forget the little tasks that keep cropping up that can easily lead to overwhelm. Then you can use the Eisenhower Matrix to decide what to do with the tasks.

Your options are:

o **Do:** Do it now because it has a deadline or it's urgent
o **Decide:** Decide what to do about it
o **Delegate:** Give it to someone else
o **Delete:** Take it off your to-do list

I like to do this in Trello because you can make a list and move the items around, but you could do this in your workbook or use a notebook and draw a simple grid too.

It stops you from working on the things that aren't important or not in your skill set so you can focus on the important and urgent tasks that you are good at.

 Use the Eisenhower Matrix in your workbook to plan out your week.

Week 4: Checklist

We've reached the end of our week all about productivity, how have you found it?

Productivity is an important tool that I know I would like to focus and improve on. How much time is wasted procrastinating or sitting behind a desk but not getting anything done?

It motivates me to work on my business, complete tasks and enjoy the time away from the screen instead!

Here are our tasks for this week for you to tick off.

☐ Find an accountability partner
☐ Notice when you're getting distracted
☐ The productivity tools that will help you
☐ Try the Pomodoro® Technique
☐ Plan how long each of your tasks will take
☐ Try getting into a deep work zone
☐ Use the Eisenhower Matrix to plan your week

Month 1 check in: How are you getting on with your goals?

We've made it to the end of the first 4 weeks! How are you feeling about your marketing?

Now is a great time to check in with those goals we set at the start of the month to see how you're getting on.

You might be finding that as we work through these tasks there is a time of day that feels like the best opportunity for you to focus. If you're noticing there is a period when you are more productive, see if you can block it out in your diary each day to work on your marketing and make it part of your routine.

There's lots of different advice about how long it takes to form a habit, but if you are working on your marketing everyday for 90 days then it's likely it will have become part of your process and how you work on your business.

Before we move onto month two, here are some questions to ask yourself to help you check in with your progress.

Have you moved forward in your business?

Take a look at some of the areas we've covered this month to see if you have moved forward in your business. They might be small steps like starting to pitch for PR opportunities or having a bank of content for the first time, but these are all moving forward!

Which goals are you putting off?

When you look at your goals is there a goal or action step that you're putting off or procrastinating on? Try and do this one next to get it out of the way or adapt the action steps to make them easier to complete. Your goals should feel exciting and achievable, if you can't see the steps leading to the goal it could be time to reassess it.

Have you been able to fit these tasks into the time you have?

It's no problem if life is busier than you expected for these 90 days and you're not finding much time to work on the tasks. Just try to do something each day to help your business. Sometimes reading the prompts is enough to spark a new idea for an offer or a post. Keep reading and come back to the ones you need to spend more time on.

Are you getting distracted?

If you're getting distracted, first try using the tools in productivity week to stay on track. If that's not working, try turning this book into a game. Give yourself a treat for the highest daily streak of completing tasks, set yourself a challenge of how many you can tick off in a day or get a reward each month for getting them done. I'm not against bribing yourself if it means you're going to improve your marketing, you need to do what works for you!

Month 2

Week 5: Graphic design – Having a consistent brand for your business

Welcome to branding and graphic design week! You might be thinking, but Hannah, you aren't a graphic designer. And you'd be correct.

Which is why I've asked my friend Liz Mosley to share her wisdom with us. Liz works with small businesses on branding and design services to help them feel more confident about sharing what they do. She hosts a great podcast called *Building Your Brand* which has lots of amazing guests talking about their experience of running a business. Don't worry, you're in good hands this week.

Day 29: Gather up all your branding

Your first task is to gather up everything you have for your branding. Whether you're just getting started or you've been using your brand for a long time, now you can bring it all together. We're looking at collecting things like

o Logos
o Colour codes
o Templates
o Style guides
o Fonts you like to use

When you've got it all, find a place to store them so you can access them easily and always have your branding to hand. It's similar to PR week when you created your folder, but this will contain all of your brand assets and make them easier to find and use. This will also help you to be more consistent because your branding is there ready to put into action.

When you've sorted out your folder, take a look and see if there are any gaps that you'd like to fill.

o Do you need a logo or want to update your current one?
o Are you using different colours each time?
o Are the fonts you used a few years ago not a good fit for your business now?

Be honest with yourself about where your branding might be holding you back in your business and what needs to change.

Day 30: Create a mood board for your brand

Today we are going to go back to basics with your branding. Branding can help people have a connection to your business, but it might have been awhile since you thought about what you want that connection to be.

First of all, write down how you want people to feel when they interact with your brand. What words come up for you and which brands do you also connect that feeling with? Does your current branding reflect that? If not, start collecting inspiration to help you work out what tweaks you could do to make sure it is communicating that feeling.

Start off by gathering images that inspire you and reflect how you want people to feel about your brand. It doesn't have to be images of logos and design – it can be anything, a word, a photograph, a pattern, a texture, an outfit, the way a room is decorated.

Some good places to look for inspiration are Pinterest, Behance, Instagram and Dribbble. You can add them to your own boards or screenshot them and save them in a folder. When you have a selection of images saved your task is to create a mood board using those images.

Use a tool like Canva or Adobe Express which are online design, photo and video tools that you can use to make social media graphics and other design assets. Both of these options have lots of mood board templates you can use.

Becca from Stiwdio Mizzi-Harris is one of our online members and said that branding week came at the perfect time as it was something she was planning to work on.

She created a brand mood board using the tasks from this week to help her narrow down her brand foundations including mission, visions, values and logo possibilities. Doing these tasks helped her to feel more confident posting online and sharing content that would appeal to her ideal clients. She wanted to have a brand that she felt reflected her, her business and clients, and now that's what she has!

Once your mood board is complete, spend a few minutes comparing it to your current branding and think about what tweaks you could make to bring your branding more in line with the mood board and yourself. Is there anything you could put into action today?

Day 31: Refresh your brand colours

Today's task is to think about your colour palette. Are you happy with the colours you're using or could they do with a refresh?

Think back to day 30 and how you said you want people to feel when they interact with your brand. Look back to your mood board, do your colours help to convey that feeling?

If you're happy with how your colours look then your task is to write down all of the hex codes of your colours and keep them somewhere safe, you'll need them again later in the week. The hex codes are numbers used to identify the colours and there are plenty of websites you can use to find the codes for your brand colours.

If you think your colours could do with some tweaking then this is your chance to have a play around. Liz recommends not changing your colours completely but you might find that adding or taking away some colours could help.

Look at your mood board for inspiration for these colours. You can use the pipette tool in Canva or Adobe Express to find the hex codes from colours in the images on your mood board.

You ideally want to have a primary brand colour and some accent colours that complement each other. You also want to make sure that you have colours that when used together on your website or social media posts will have enough contrast.

You can use an accessibility website to check how legible words will be using different colours, just input the background colour hex code and the writing hex code and it will give you the score. You can also find colour palette suggestions and inspiration on the other pages of the website.

This is all about making sure your colours are working for you so give yourself some time to look at what could be improved!

Write down the hex codes for your brand colours.

Day 32: Find your font names

Today we are going to be thinking about your typography. What fonts are you currently using in your branding? Your first task is to make a list of your font names. If you aren't sure what fonts you're using on your website you can use a Chrome plugin called WhatFont, simply scroll over a font and it will tell you what it's called.

Ideally you want to have a heading font and a body copy font. They can be the same but the body copy font needs to be something very simple and readable, the heading font can be more exciting but still needs to be easy to read.

You might also want to have an accent font that is more ornate and interesting but is used sparingly as these are often harder to read.

Again, fonts can have a lot of personality and convey lots of information so think back to how you want people to feel when they interact with your brand and make sure your font choice is aligned with that.

If you need inspiration take a look at some other brands to see the difference in the fonts they're using.

Once you're happy with your font choices, make a note of them with your colour hex codes. Your brand guidelines are starting to take shape!

 Write down the names of the fonts you use for your brand.

Day 33: Decide if you're happy with your current logo

Today you are going to have a look at the logo files you have. You will typically need the following as a minimum:

o   A png with a transparent background to use online
o   A high-resolution jpeg that you can use for print

o   If you have a vector eps version of your logo this is also really helpful

If you already have these files of your logo, put all the different variations and colour options in a folder together so that they are easy for you to find and use. It would be useful to have these in your PR folder too.

While you are doing this you can also reflect on whether you are happy with your logo and if it's suitable for use in the ways that you need.

o   Is it responsive?
o   Do you have smaller versions that work on social media?
o   Do you have larger versions that work on your website banner or on printed items?
o   Is getting a new logo something you want to invest in or are you happy with what you currently have?

This week is all about reflecting on your branding and noticing where there are tweaks to be made, feeling confident about the parts you are happy with or knowing when is the right time to start again and create something new.

Day 34: Create a simple brand guidelines document

For today's task you are going to put together a simple brand guidelines document that should include all of the information that you have been collecting throughout the week.

Start by taking a look on Canva or Adobe Express and finding one of their brand guidelines templates. Add in all of the information we have been collecting over the last few days and see your brand guidelines start to take shape!

When you've filled in the template, save it as a PDF, keep it in the folder with all of your logo file formats and store it somewhere handy that is easy to find and access.

This is also a great document to use if you ever outsource some of your design work or bring another team member into your business. They will be able to access everything from one place and keep their work consistent with your branding.

Your brand guidelines are there for you to put into practice, so add in any information you would find useful too!

Day 35: Ask clients what they think

It's our final task for branding week, how have you found this week? Hopefully it has helped you either make some improvements to your branding or confirm that you're on the right track with it. It's always good to make sure you have everything you need and can access it easily.

Your final task for this week is to ask some of your customers and clients what they think about your branding.

You could use some of the survey tools we used in week 2 to find out what they feel when they see your logo and brand colours, what emotions come up and what other businesses they might compare it to.

This task is only for you if you're ready to hear some honest feedback! But it will be useful feedback to receive.

Thank you to Liz for the tasks for this week, I really hope they have helped you to think more about your branding and quick and simple ways you can improve it.

Week 5: Checklist

As a small business owner, branding is something you might get stuck on and stop you moving forward in your business.

Having clear guidelines to follow makes other parts of your business simpler too. You can create consistent graphics, have a website that feels like you and your brand is easier to recognize by your customers.

It's well worth spending some time on this or working with a professional to help create a brand that you're really proud of.

Here are your tasks to get you started:

☐ Gather up all your branding
☐ Create a mood board for your brand
☐ Refresh your brand colours
☐ Find your font names
☐ Decide if you're happy with your current logo
☐ Create a simple brand guidelines document
☐ Ask clients what they think

Week 6: Website and search engine optimization (SEO) – Get more potential customers to visit your website

Your website might be the first point of contact that a potential customer has with your business, or it could be the last point before they are about to make a purchase. It's important to get it right.

These 10-minute tasks will guide you to improve your current website and work on your SEO to help more potential customers find you through a search engine. When your audience are searching for specific words and phrases online, you want to be the website that they click on and one of the ways we can improve that is with your online content.

Before we begin website and SEO week, I'd like to say that I'm not an SEO expert. The tips in this chapter are things I have tried out for myself or picked up along the way. There are plenty of ways you can improve your SEO, but if it's something you would like to focus on I would recommend speaking to someone that specializes in it.

This book is designed to give you a taster of the different marketing tools available and there might be some that you want to get some further expertise or do your own research on. As with all of these prompts, take what you need and leave the rest.

Day 36: Check your website is up to date

Let's start things off with an easy task for website week. Does your website feel like it fits the season we're in now?

It's really important that when a customer or potential client clicks on your website, they know that they are in the right place and they've found someone that can help them. A website that is out of date doesn't show that you're still in business and have available services.

If it's March and your business is still showing your Christmas products, it's time to update it. If it's November and there's no sign of festivities, how will people know you have amazing products for sale?

Does your website mention the season at all? If you're launching something new does it link to how someone is feeling right now? This is really important for product-based businesses, but it can be useful for service businesses too.

Every time I launch The Best 90 Days Ever online membership, I make sure the colours I use will fit the season we're in. Our October launch has lots of orange and autumnal colours, our summer launch is bright with yellows and blues.

Your website can show your customers that you know how they're feeling right now and you have a product or service that's going to help them. Subtly showing the season we're in is a really easy way to do that and it can be as simple as updating a headline on your home page.

If you're struggling with this, ask someone to take a look at your website and give you some feedback on how it could feel more up to date.

Day 37: Make a list of the keywords to use

Today's task is to think about what makes you and your website different and use that information to choose and write down your keywords.

Keywords are the words that your ideal clients would search on Google to find you. They could be individual words or a few words together, but they are specific to you and your business.

Start writing down a list of the words that people might use to describe your business or find you online. Mine could be:

o   Hannah Isted
o   HI Communications
o   The Best 90 Days Ever
o   Author
o   Marketing
o   Barry
o   South Wales
o   Social media
o   Small business

These are all some of the words I would feature on my website and in my blog posts to increase the chances of my target audience finding me online.

Here is an example for one of my favourite local businesses in Barry, an Italian restaurant that we're getting married at.

If you just searched 'pizza restaurant' online to try and find it, the search would be too vague. I wonder how many pizza restaurants there are in the world!

But if you searched – authentic pizza restaurant in Barry, you would have a more specific search. Start to think about where you can reverse this process, take those specific words and add them into the copy on your website.

Ironically when you search our local pizza restaurant my blog post comes up because of the keywords in an article I wrote about them years ago.

Your aim for this task is to find out what those keywords are and feature them in your blog content and in other areas on your website.

Online member, Jon Evans, who I mentioned in our mind map task said:

> *The SEO weeks have really helped me, they are a great introduction into what I thought was a techie subject but actually isn't. You made it easy to make tangible changes and now I have a bit of a standard for myself to make sure I get keywords in and images are well documented with alt text! It's made me now rank first for smaller uncompetitive terms but the most proud I am is third for a very popular term "Couch to 5k tips".'*

Write down some keywords that you would like your ideal clients to search to find your website.

Think about things like location, services, personality, anything that stands out about you. You can also do this task if you don't have a website yet and get ahead of the game with your SEO!

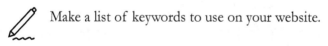 Make a list of keywords to use on your website.

Day 38: Tick off the quick website checklist

Today's task is a checklist that you can run through with a list of tasks for your website that are often forgotten. These are useful to check over every few months and they can give you an easy win if you want to make new updates.

This is one of those tasks where it should only take 10 minutes to check the list, but if any of them are broken you might need some extra time to fix the problem.

Set a timer for 10 minutes, open up your website and get working!

- ☐ Is your copyright at the bottom of the page showing the current year?
- ☐ Have you removed all traces of previous seasons and promotions?
- ☐ Do your social media links work?
- ☐ Is your email sign up form working?
- ☐ Is your Favicon correct? (this is the little image that shows up on the internet tab)
- ☐ Do you have all your policies and terms and conditions in place?
- ☐ Is your shop working? Can people buy from you?

If you've noticed your sales have dropped or you aren't getting as many sign-ups for your email newsletter, it could be something simple like a website form isn't working properly.

These are useful things to check and keep on top of to make sure your website is running smoothly.

Day 39: Update your website backlinks

If I say the word 'backlinks' do you:

A. Look at me blankly because you don't know what I'm talking about

B. Know what they are but haven't done much work on them

C. Feel smug because you can probably skip this task!

To keep it simple, backlinks are where you link to other people's websites from your own, or you have a link going to your website from somewhere else. These are brilliant for SEO and not as complicated as they might sound.

Think about the places on the internet where you display your website link. Instagram? Pinterest? Facebook? Etsy? LinkedIn? Online directories?

Go back and check that you've added the correct website to all of these different places and see if there is anywhere else you can add too.

Do you have any blog posts that feature other businesses? If not, it could be a good idea to start creating them or see if you can connect with other people to collaborate and share their website too.

You could create your own directory page of recommended suppliers with links or add in a link to your clients and show a case study of them.

We are going to look into this more over the next couple of chapters, but start with the task of checking your current backlinks and let's go from there.

Day 40: Optimize your website images

Today's task is about the images on your website. The images you use on your website and across social media are important and you should make sure that you have the correct permission to use them.

The ideal solution is to take your own photos or use a photographer, but there are websites that provide copyright-free images, just make sure you're able to use them for a business.

Many small business owners focus on having beautiful images on their website, but this can often mean they have minimal text which isn't improving their SEO.

If you have lots of lovely graphics filled with words, those words aren't going to get recognized and they won't be searchable. If they aren't searchable, they aren't helping your website get found.

As well as adding more text to your website, one way to improve your search results is to optimize your images so they are working harder for you.

We can make sure our images are searchable by using Alternative Text (alt text) to tell the search engines what is in that image. The text can appear if the image doesn't load and is also really important for accessibility and for someone who might use software to describe the image.

All of our images should have a good description but it needs to be accurate, we don't just want to chuck a load of words in for the sake of it.

Today's task is to find a page on your website and check the images have a description and alt text. Going forward it's also good to name your images before you upload them to your website too.

I will say that this is one thing I struggle with and often forget to do. When you are in a rush it can be something I miss off the list but I am going back over my previous content to improve it.

Day 41: Check your website on mobile

Today's task is a very quick task but also extremely important. Your task is to check your website on the mobile version and on iPad too. Many (if not most!) of your customers will visit your website on their phone and it needs to work well.

Look through each page on your website, including the checkout if you have a shop, and see if there's anything that needs to be changed, updated or removed.

o   Is the font size okay?
o   Do the images fit on the screen?
o   Can you tell what you do from the first page?

Make sure that whenever you update your website you check the mobile version too as it's easy to make edits that will affect the rest of your pages.

If you outsource your website changes you can still check through each of your pages and ask your web developer to make the edits for you.

Day 42: Start planning a collaboration blog post

For our final task for website and SEO week, I want you to think of a blog post idea that is going to drive traffic to your website.

Our next chapter is all about collaborating so your mission, should you choose to accept it, is to plan an amazing blog post that includes other businesses.

Think about a topic that includes the keywords that we worked on at the start of this week. You might want to consider how you could involve your local area if you want to focus on local keywords. Or you could choose some of the keywords related to your industry such as 'small business' and make a list of all the small businesses that you would love to get involved with for your blog project. Find their contact details or start planning a visit if you can.

Here are some examples that I would do which would still fit my business but also be good for my website SEO.

Location: The five most productive co-working spaces for small businesses in South Wales; Three of the best small business owners you need to visit in Barry; Events not to miss for small business owners in Cardiff this summer.

Keywords: Eight members of The Best 90 Days Ever share their top marketing tips; The Best 90 Days Ever member of the month Q&A (you can read these on my website!); Why these ten small business owners joined The Best 90 Days Ever.

Seasonal: Five small business owners share how they're promoting their business over Christmas; How to show small businesses love this Valentine's Day; How to use Halloween for your small business marketing.

Harriet is an online member and runs Below the Line Finance, she has been using the tips from blogging week to help her connect with her audience. Here's what she says about them!

I had always known the significance of blogging for my website, but I used to believe it would consume hours of my time and would be too challenging to keep up with — so I didn't do it! However, Hannah's approach simplifies the writing process and it still amazes me how fast I can now create and share really helpful blog posts.

What's even better is that I frequently receive messages from people about my blogs. I'm delighted to have found a consistent way to write them and it's really helped me connect with my audience.

Additionally, I find it great to start with a blog post and then repurpose the content for my newsletter and social media posts. It's incredibly versatile and saves me so much time.

Remember the task for today is just to come up with the plan or the title, then you're going to start gathering up the information during blogging week and finally you're going to write it.

Write down three ideas for your collaboration blog posts.

Week 6: Checklist

Hopefully this week has helped you to start thinking about ways you can maximize the words and space on your website. You only get one chance to make a first impression so keep working on your website to get it right.

Feedback from your ideal clients and customers can be really useful, especially if you're not sure if you're using the same language that they would be using. Create a survey to ask for feedback on the way your website looks and the words you've used and see where it could be improved to appeal more to your target audience.

Here are your tasks to tick off:

☐ Check your website is up to date
☐ Make a list of the keywords to use
☐ Tick off the quick website checklist
☐ Update your website backlinks
☐ Optimize your website images
☐ Check your website on mobile
☐ Start planning a collaboration blog

Week 7: Collaborating – How to team up with other business owners

Being self-employed has its pros and cons, but one of those pros is definitely working together with other business owners.

You can create some amazing relationships that benefit everyone involved, whether that's helping with your marketing, exploring new ideas or getting together for events. They say that teamwork makes the dream work and I really think that's true.

Collaboration week has been one of the most popular weeks in The Best 90 Days Ever online membership because we have so many supportive members in the group that love to work together. I think the community is one of the main reasons people join, it's not always easy to find a group that helps each other this much.

Although I can't bring that exact community to this book, I hope that these prompts will give you some ideas and inspiration so you can find that community and ways to collaborate for yourself.

Day 43: Start sending your collaboration emails

Let's pick up where you left SEO week, putting together an idea for a blog post that collaborates with other businesses for our website.

This week we're going straight into collaborating week and I'm throwing you in at the deep end. Your task for today is to make the list of people you'd like to include in that blog post and start approaching them.

Put together a short email that says what you're doing, how it will benefit them with backlinks and social media shares and what they need to do to be included. You might want them to send over a few paragraphs, a high-resolution image that you have permission to use and links to their website and social media accounts.

As someone who has contributed to a few blog posts, a word count is really useful here. If you're not sure, write out your own example paragraph and check the word count for that length of text.

When you're sending the email make sure you give a deadline. This means they can decline if it's going to be too short notice for them and they know when you're expecting to receive the content and make it live on your website.

If you don't have a blog on your website or you're in the process of creating or updating your website, you could also do this as a carousel post on social media or share it in your newsletter.

Start sending out those emails or direct messages and see who replies!

If you find that you're not getting many responses, it might be that you need to do some relationship building first but keep trying and don't give up with this.

Day 44: Share a post and tag a business

One of the easiest ways to support other small business owners to reach a wider audience is by sharing their content and social media accounts. Today's task is a fun one, share a post that you can tag another business in.

This is such a simple and free way to help other business owners and it feels so good when someone else does this in return for you. We've all seen those posts about ways to support businesses for free, today it's time to put it into action!

Here are some examples if you need inspiration:

O   It could be heading out for a coffee and tagging the local cafe
O   Another business you've worked with on a project
O   A podcast you love and recommend
O   A graphic or meme you relate to that they posted
O   One of the people you put on your pitching list

You can do this on your Instagram stories or create a grid post. If you can get into the habit of sharing and connecting with others it helps us to be seen as a part of that community and can often get you noticed by those businesses which is great for building relationships.

Try it today and see what results you get, at the very least it will make them happy, but you never know, it could spark a new conversation!

Day 45: Pick an area that you want to collaborate

You're halfway through *The Best 90 Days Ever*! Well done everyone for getting this far.

Please don't stress if you feel behind. Just do what you can with the time and energy that you have.

Even reading the tasks each day and doing a few here and there is worth it. *You've got this.*

Today's task is to pick an area of your business or marketing and look at how collaborating might benefit that area. If you're feeling stuck with your marketing it might be because you're doing the same type of activities on repeat and it's time to mix it up. Collaborations help you to expand to reach new people that you might not have been able to on your own.

Here are some suggestions for areas you could collaborate in:

o   If you have a podcast and you want to reach a wider audience, you could look at finding some new guests for interviews or pitch to be on podcasts yourself.

o   If you run a membership group and there is a gap in your knowledge you could swap with another business owner to speak in each other's groups.

o   If you want to grow your Instagram account you could collaborate with another business on a grid post or a live video.

o   If you want to try something new you could team up with a business for a live event and create something amazing that people really want to come to.

Businesses big and small team up all the time for collaborations. Look at where you want to improve your business and think about how a collaboration could help with that.

Day 46: Find someone to collaborate with

Today's task is to find someone that you can collaborate with. We've already spoken about collaborating with a blog post, but there are so many other ways you can team up to benefit your marketing.

Here are a few ideas:

o You might find that you are in the same field and can put together a really useful post on LinkedIn or Instagram.

o Plan a Facebook or Instagram live together on a topic that is relevant for both of your businesses.

o Design a carousel post featuring multiple businesses that you can tag.

o Write a blog post for each other's websites. You could make a two-part series where part one is on one blog and part two is on the other.

o Record a podcast together. I have been a guest on Liz's podcast (our expert from design week) and she has been a guest for 6 weeks on my podcast *The Social Sunday* for a summer season.

o Team up for a product collection. Take inspiration from some of big businesses on how they do this. Look at new films and see all the product collaborations that come with them.

o Find someone to test your new service, you'll get the feedback and they could get the service for free or at a beta price.

o Team up with an influencer. Research someone that you'd like to send your product to and find out about their prices for content.

There are so many ways to collaborate with other business owners. See if you can find a connection you have that could benefit each other.

 Write down some ways you want to collaborate with other businesses.

Day 47: Set up Tea Break Chats

Today's task is to set up some Tea Break Chats! Tea Break Chats are short 15-minute catch ups online where you can ask a specific question, look for advice or just get to know each other. We do these in The Best 90 Days Ever membership and they have always been really helpful for those times when you have an idea and you need to ask someone outside of your business for their opinion.

To set up some Tea Break Chats you could write a post on social media, say when you're available and invite people to chat with you.

You might find that someone has a totally different view of your business and it sparks an idea for a social media post, a blog post or even a lead magnet you could use. They could be a previous customer and give you some great feedback on how you could improve your offer.

I'd recommend setting a timer for these conversations so you both know where you stand with the time and don't get carried away. The aim is that they are short and sweet and I'd really recommend seeing if you can fit a few in.

Tea Break Chats are meant to help both people taking part so make sure this is mutually beneficial for everyone and you both get a chance to talk.

Day 48: Create an in-person collaboration

You've spent most of these 90 days online, so let's take this off the internet for today's task and think about an in-person collaboration.

I've noticed the popularity for in-person events and experiences is increasing and for small business owners who work on their own it can be great to get together and meet new people.

An in-person event can be big or small so think about the type of event you could team up with someone to organize. Here are some ideas.

Workshops: Pick a topic you can both discuss and plan an in-person workshop where there is a clear outcome. I run in-person workshops on batch creating where the aim is to get your content created.

I have also run an event with Liz Mosley where I'll talk about batching creating the caption and she will explain how to make the graphics and templates to go with them. It works really well because our skills complement each other and we have similar but different audiences. The event can be free or paid and could be used as a way to grow your audience and give you some great content too.

Share a shop: Taking on a whole shop can be a big risk for some business owners who just want to test the waters, so why not see if you can collaborate with one or multiple businesses to open your own space? Pop-up shops are everywhere, see if there are any schemes in your local area to help.

Local community events: Are there any events in your local area that you could help with or have a stall at? If your target audience is local this can be a great way to get your name out there and you might have a skill that will benefit the event and help it reach more people.

You could also organize a local networking event to bring together other business owners. We have previously organized Barry Business Club meetings and it was great to bring people to meet each other in one room.

Other events: There are so many other events that you could plan a collaboration for, such as free talks, outdoor events and even activities like shopping nights and wine tastings. Think about what your target audience would like to attend and contact some business owners that you'd love to team up with.

This is always a reminder for me that my business isn't just online and those in-person events really help to grow your audience and in a lot of cases, turn clients and customers into friends.

Day 49: What do you bring to the table for collaborating?

Your final task for collaboration week is to think about what you bring to the table for a collaboration.

When you team up with another business it should be mutually beneficial for you both, but that doesn't mean you have to have a huge audience or a massive mailing list.

You might have a unique view on something that is a good match for their website. You might be prepared to take on all the organizing for the collaboration so all they have to do is pop a blog on their website or accept a collaboration on a post.

You might have an audience that they haven't been able to reach before but would be great for them.

Give yourself a quick boost today and write down five things you bring to the table for your next collaboration. Your business is unique and that needs to be celebrated!

 Write down five things you could bring to your next collaboration.

Week 7: Checklist

I hope you've enjoyed collaboration week. This is always a popular week inside the online membership because we all team up with each other to connect and collaborate together.

Collaborating with other businesses can be loads of fun and it's helped me to meet so many new people along the way that I might not have met otherwise.

See how you can add some collaborations into your marketing plan across the year and give yourself plenty of time to get working on them.

Your checklist is here to get you started:

- ☐ Start sending your collaboration emails
- ☐ Share a post and tag a business
- ☐ Pick an area that you want to collaborate
- ☐ Find someone to collaborate with
- ☐ Set up Tea Break Chats
- ☐ Create an in-person collaboration
- ☐ What do you bring to the table for collaborating?

Week 8: Blogging – Why blogging is great for boosting your website

I can't believe we are over halfway through having *The Best 90 Days Ever!* For the next 7 days we're going to be looking at blogging.

Even when algorithms change and new social media platforms are created, having a blog on your website is always a good way to bring in new traffic and help you to show up higher for search terms on Google.

Not only that, it's a great way to create some long form content that you can reuse across different platforms. It's almost like a big storage solution for some of your best content, so that you can come back to it and pick and choose what to use again.

It shows you're an expert in your industry and as we spoke about in the previous week, it's a great way to collaborate with other businesses and form relationships too.

During lockdown I spent lots of time working on the blog on my website and sharing those blog posts on Pinterest. It helped my SEO so much and those blogs and pins are still being found and read today. I would love to make it a focus in my marketing plan again.

The goal for the end of this week is to have ideas for blog posts and start writing at least one. If you don't have a website yet or a space to share your blog posts, you can still create this content and share it on LinkedIn or another content sharing website.

Day 50: Write the first 100 words of your blog post

Welcome to Blogging Week, this week I'm going to mix it up a little and set you a challenge. Your main task for this week is to write a blog post and get it up on your website.

I'm hoping we have set the groundwork from our SEO and collaborating weeks by gathering up some content that you can use for your blog post. If you are still waiting to hear back from people who are featuring in your blog, now is the time to chase them.

If that's not your aim for this week, you can also create your own individual blog post on a relevant topic which we will be covering over the next few days.

I'd recommend having a minimum goal of 500 words for your blog posts, but this week we're going to aim for 700 words and split them up each day. You can definitely write more for your blog posts but I want to make this achievable over the week and break it down in a way that will fit into the rest of your day.

You can do this – just write 700 words minimum, 100 words a day. Easy.

If you don't have a blog on your website or you are a frequent blogger and this isn't much of a challenge, think about how you can change this to a more difficult task. You might want to try a different type of blog post this week or explore where you can share long form content that isn't on your website.

For today, just write that first 100 words of your collaboration blog post and get the ball rolling. Your blog post should have an introduction so this is a great place to start. Tell us what your blog post is going to be about, how it will help and why we should read it. Good luck!

Day 51: Go on a treasure hunt for words

Today's task is to go on a treasure hunt for words you've already written. This book is all about saving you time on your marketing. I'm not going to ask you to write content from scratch if you know you've already created another piece of content that you could reuse. Today is all about finding those words and looking at ways you can repurpose them.

Blogs don't have to be made up of completely new words. You can reuse content you've already written or even videos you've recorded in the past.

Here are some places you could look for content to turn into blog posts:

o   Instagram posts, especially numbered carousels
o   Notes or slides from a workshop
o   Podcast notes you've written before recording
o   Transcripts from podcasts, webinars, live videos
o   Newsletters and email series
o   Blog posts you've already written that can be recreated
o   Collaborations you've done with other businesses

One of my favourite ways to reuse this content is to turn it into a 'listicle'. A listicle is a piece of content that is in the form of a numbered list. It's similar to the 'five ways' post we created, but this one is going to include more information. The number is up to you, so don't feel pressured to come up with 50 ideas when it could just be five!

Some examples of these for my business could be:

o   Fifteen content ideas for your small business this summer
o   Five ways to reuse your content for social media
o   Ten small business podcasts you should listen to today

Listicles work well when you are reusing content because they are a great way to bring together other posts into one consistent article. You could pick five of the best tips you've shared on social media, or look through your old newsletters and see if there are 18 ideas from there.

Make the most of the words you're writing in other places and get them up on your blog too.

While you're there, write another 100 words of your new blog post please!

Day 52: Update the call to action on your blogs

If you already have blogs up on your website, don't waste a valuable opportunity to keep hold of your audience's attention after they've finished reading.

Instead, go back and update those previous blog posts with new links and information. Think about what the topic of the blog post is and what the next natural step for someone would be after they have finished reading it. This is the call to action and the next move you want them to make when they've read it.

Some of your blogs might naturally promote an offer that you have, in fact that might have been why you wrote that blog post in the first place.

It could be that the blog is a good way to encourage people to join your email list after they've read it. But how will they know if you don't tell them? At the end of each blog think – what next?

Pick a few of your most popular blog posts and go through this checklist:

o   Is there anything that can be improved or updated?
o   Are the links broken or still accurate?
o   Can this link to a new course or a product?
o   Do they go to a landing page with an email sign up?

If they enjoy the blog and want to read more, don't waste that opportunity to give them the next step.

Oh, and before I forget, write another 100 words of your blog post please!

Day 53: Narrow down your list of topics

Getting started with writing blogs can feel hard, because we can potentially write about anything on our website. But if you're going to put time and effort into writing that blog post, it should have a role to play in your marketing.

Today's task is about narrowing down what you're going to write about in your blogs so that it will have a positive impact on your SEO and create a list of topics you can come back to across the year.

To start, go back to week 6, website and SEO week and look at those main keywords you picked out for your website that you want people to be searching to find you.

Then take a look back at your mind map from week 2, Batch Creating Week, and see what you could turn into a blog or an article. There will be connections between the words and phrases that you can use to create blog posts.

The final thing to consider when planning your blogs is what your audience is searching for right now. They might be looking for ideas for summer, Halloween activities or gifts to buy at Christmas. Seasonal themes can really give your blog a focus and narrow down wider topics to make them more specific.

Here are some questions to ask:

o   What do you want people to search for to find you?
o   Which topics can you frequently talk or write about?
o   What can you give your expertise on?
o   What are your audience searching for this season?

For example, I want people to start to find my website when they are planning a launch or writing content and wondering how to use Trello, because I know that my Trello templates will help them.

That's already an idea for several blog posts that I can create to encourage people to find me using keywords relating to Trello and launching.

If you're struggling, ask your audience and see if they can help to give you some ideas for the topics you want to write about. Don't forget to take a look over those surveys and poll questions you did in week two as well.

Of course, I couldn't let you get away without asking you to write another 100 words of your blog post please!

Day 54: Use Google autofill for blog suggestions

This is a nice easy task if you have 5 minutes today and want to build on that bank of blog post ideas we started yesterday.

Get on Google and use Google autofill to give you some inspiration for blog posts. You'll notice that when you start to type a topic or idea it will autofill suggestions for you based on what other people are searching.

Note down what the suggestions are and how you would answer them with your content. If you have no idea what to write about, start typing a phrase related to your industry.

Things like:

o   Why does…
o   How do you create…
o   What is the difference between…
o   What is the easiest way to…

Then look at the suggestions from Google. Are these things you could write about or give expertise on?

If someone is searching for them it's because they are interested in finding out more, so write a related blog post and give them the answers they are looking for.

There are other tools that are gaining popularity as I'm writing this book such as ChatGPT so if you would prefer to use one of those, take this prompt and see what is available to help spark some more ideas.

How is your list of blog post ideas looking? If you're not sure which one to start writing next you could select your top four and ask your audience to pick which one they would like to read first. I like to do this in an Instagram story with a poll sticker so they can vote. It helps them to feel more involved in the process and hopefully more likely to read it too.

Don't forget to write that next 100 words of your blog post… you're almost there!

 Write down five suggested ideas for your next blog post.

Day 55: Create a writing habit

Today's task is to create a writing habit. In the book *The Artist's Way*, Julia Cameron talks about writing daily 'morning pages' which is free writing about anything that's on your mind. It's really good for getting into the habit of writing and also having a routine that helps you to be more creative.

If writing a blog post feels like a big task for you because it's a larger piece of content than you're used to, it might help to start a writing routine first.

Take the pressure off writing about your business and just start free writing each day with anything that comes to mind. You can do this in your journal or you could do it on your laptop or phone.

When you've created that habit, see if you can switch it to writing about business. Even just 10 minutes each day can be enough to create a couple of social media posts, or write part of a newsletter or blog that you could share later.

Try to create a writing habit that helps you to get into the routine of writing daily.

You might have noticed that during this week I haven't suggested any specific length or format of blog, we're just aiming for a foundation of 700 words. I'll be honest, I don't want to give you any reason not to do these tasks.

When you start to decide how things 'should' look it gives you a reason to not get started because you don't think you will reach that 'should'.

Of course, there is plenty of advice out there on the best length of a blog, the best time you should be sharing it and the best way to format it. If you feel like that would be useful, I'd definitely encourage you to research it more.

But just for this week I want you to try and get ahead on your list of ideas, start creating content and building a writing habit that works for you.

Have you written those 100 words yet?

Day 56: Check where your blogs are going to go

For your final day of blogging week, I want you to look at where your blogs are going to go.

This week has been focused on sharing the blog post on your website to get the SEO benefits, but not everyone has a website.

There are still plenty of reasons to share a blog post or an article even if you aren't trying to impress Google.

They can help to show you as an expert in your industry, build your audience on social media and help to grow your community too.

Here are a few suggestions for other places you could share your writing.

o   Substack
o   Medium
o   LinkedIn
o   Facebook

When you've decided where you're going to share your blog, check that everything is up to date on that platform. Finish your final 100 words with a conclusion and call to action, and then I want you to upload it!

It might not be perfect, it might not be your finest work, but it's done and you can always come back and edit it later. Well done for getting that work out there.

Give yourself a pat on the back, you've done it!

Week 8: Checklist

Well done for getting blogging week done. It can be tough to get yourself into the mindset of writing a piece of content longer than just a social media post.

If there's one thing to take away from this book it's that everything you write and create can be reused in some way. We are all busy and if you're spending time on a piece of content you want to be able to squeeze the juice out of it and reuse it.

Challenge yourself to reuse these blog posts in as many ways as you can. Be repetitive, it's a good thing!

Tick off this checklist and keep going.

- ☐ Write the first 100 words of your blog post
- ☐ Go on a treasure hunt for words
- ☐ Update the call to action on your blogs
- ☐ Narrow down your list of topics
- ☐ Use Google autofill for blog suggestions
- ☐ Create a writing habit
- ☐ Check where your blogs are going to go

Month 2 check in: Are you still making progress?

These two months always seem to fly by and it's easy to let them pass without really acknowledging how much work has gone into them.

It's not easy to start working on your business every single day, especially if it's something you weren't used to doing before. You deserve to celebrate having the motivation to keep going and moving forward with your marketing, even when it feels tough.

Take a look back over the last 56 tasks and write down some of the things you've managed to achieve, big and small.

Did you come up with a great idea for a collaboration and meet someone new in the process?

Maybe the idea was sparked from an email you sent to them at the start of the week and you've been working on a new in-person event together. Or you tagged them in a story on Instagram and it started a conversation where they invited you to be a guest on their podcast. These small things are all worth celebrating.

Did you secure a great piece of press coverage for your business?

If you were scrolling on #JournoRequest and you found a great opportunity for your business that has led to some press, shout about it! That's something many businesses would love to achieve and you've done it all by yourself.

Are you feeling more productive? Working quicker and more efficiently?

You might be noticing that during the day you're getting more done and in a shorter amount of time. Learning the tools to be more productive can completely change the way you work. You might not realize it now, but that's something that will be really useful in the future.

These are all things to celebrate and keep in mind as you're working through this book.

As business owners it can be hard to look back at what we've achieved, especially when we're just trying to keep moving forward each day. But it's really important to pause and look back, and I'm here celebrating with you!

Month 3

Week 9: Video content – How video content can improve your messaging

L et's kick month 3 off with one of my favourite weeks, video week.

Video content has completely changed how we use social media for our businesses. Do you remember when Instagram was all about posting one square photo with a X-Pro II filter over the top?

I still remember the first ever picture I shared on 28th December 2012 of my cat Puss with the caption 'I feel like a photographer already', ironic that I would go on to marry a photographer 11 years later!

Then there were Instagram stories, lives and reels, before starting a TikTok account and wondering what to share on both platforms without creating loads of extra work for ourselves.

Of course, video content isn't just about short form content for Instagram and TikTok. You might be creating longer content for YouTube or sharing it on other platforms like LinkedIn and Facebook too.

But as these prompts are designed to take 10 minutes or less, we are generally going to be focusing on short forms of video content this week including Instagram reels and lives, TikToks and YouTube Shorts.

If you're ready to work on your video content, clean off that phone camera and let's do this!

Day 57: Start documenting your day with videos

Welcome to video week. I'm really excited for this week because I think videos can have such an impact for your business and they can be really simple to add into your marketing plan too.

Today you have two tasks, don't worry they won't take longer than 10 minutes.

The first task is to fill in the rest of this sentence and commit to doing something new with video this week.

'By the end of this week I am going to…'

You might want to:

o   Go live for the first time
o   Set up a TikTok account
o   Try a reel transition
o   Record a behind the scenes video of your day

The choice is up to you, but pick something that is going to take you out of your comfort zone.

If your goal was the final option to record a behind the scenes video, you're in luck!

That's the second task for today.

Start documenting your day with short videos throughout this week, starting right now. Where are you reading this book? What are you working on at the moment?

Take some short videos with what you're up to, behind the scenes of your business or anything that catches your eye that could be used.

Not only do these make a great video, these short snippets are easy to use individually for reels by adding text over the top with a key message.

Make the most of the video content you're taking, it doesn't need to be single use. Even as trends and platforms change there are still multiple ways you can take one piece of video and reuse it.

 Fill in the sentence 'By the end of this week I am going to…'.

Day 58: Record a different type of video

How do you feel about videos if you gave them a score out of ten? Write down your score somewhere so you can come back to it at the end of this week and let's see if you can improve it.

You want to have something to base your score on, so let's get video week off to a good start by recording a video!

When was the last time you used video content in your marketing? Video can be used across all of your social media channels, your newsletter, your blog and your website. The more you use it, the better you'll get at it.

I set myself a ridiculous challenge this year to post 500 TikTok videos. I'm writing this in July and let's just say I am definitely not on track to complete the challenge, far from it. But even though I gave up pretty early I did notice that it already had a big impact on the quality of the rest of my videos and my creativity.

To get better at something most of us need to be practicing it. The aim with my challenge wasn't to share 500 fantastic videos, it was to share 500 videos of anything at all. After a week of posting daily videos I noticed they were getting better and better which translated to more engagement across my Instagram videos too.

Now I'm not suggesting you have to also set a silly challenge you're unlikely to complete. But today is an opportunity to try something you might not have tried before.

You don't need to show your face or do a transition if you're not ready but you could push yourself out of your comfort zone this week.

Here are a few options for your task for today, or feel free to create your own depending on what your goals are.

o   Record an Instagram story
o   Record a reel
o   Go live on Instagram
o   Go live on Facebook
o   Film your products
o   Film a tutorial for your website
o   Record an interview
o   Film a YouTube video

Which one are you going to do? Remember these are meant to be fun but challenging. If you aren't enjoying the task you've picked, scrap it and choose something else!

Day 59: Film a live video or prepare for one

Today is all about live videos. When you hear that phrase how do you feel? Some people are filled with dread at the thought of going live, others don't mind it at all. Have you done a live video before? You can do a live video on Facebook, Instagram and TikTok and today's task is to get you ready.

Live videos are great for going into more detail about an offer or a topic of conversation and they are brilliant for collaborating with another business and expanding both of your audiences.

I actually really enjoy doing live videos, on my own and with other people. If you can do a live video with someone that you have a connection with it can make for a really interesting conversation.

I also find that they make up a key part of a launch plan when I'm promoting The Best 90 Days Ever membership. If you are comfortable talking about a topic, a live video is a good way to describe it in more detail, in a way that feels natural for you. You can answer questions anyone has while you're live on air which is great if a few people have similar questions.

When I do a live video about the membership I nearly always see a spike in visits to my website and sales.

One of our online members, Sian, who runs SC Fitness said:

I never had the confidence to do this in the past but was determined to give this task a go as I know as a consumer that I find live videos very engaging. I decided to film some videos on my Instagram stories to help promote my coaching service and I had so many messages in response. I realized how going live shows me at my most authentic self, in an unedited way which is what people relate to. It was a great way to start some conversations and keep my followers interested in my content.

This week I want you to feel ready for a live video, and there are lots of different ways to do this depending on what stage you're at.

If you've never done a live video before you can start by:

o   Recording what you want to say first on your phone's front camera. This will help you get used to watching yourself talk and not getting too distracted by your own face! The first time you do a live it can feel strange to see yourself. This will help to take the uncomfortableness away.

o   When you're happy with that, try doing a Facetime with a supportive friend to practice. You might get the giggles seeing them there but it helps you to say what you need to say in front of an audience. I actually find this harder than just going live so only do this if it works for you!

o Write notes to have with you. Don't feel like you can't have any notes with you for your live video, but I would recommend only having them there if you really need them so you aren't tempted to keep looking down. I always write out a few bullet points, but for me just the act of writing them helps me to remember what I need to say.

o Using the 'practice' mode on Instagram, this can really help if you're worried about the tech or anxious about the unknown! This is a great feature that our members have loved when I've showed them. When you go to do a live on Instagram there is the option to change the audience to a practice audience. This means you can go through all the steps of going live, speaking to the screen and ending the live without having to do it in front of anyone.

o If you're very nervous, try doing it at a time where not many people are online. When you click on the live button it will tell you how many of your followers are live at that time. For your first one you could try it at a time that won't be as popular like early morning or late at night.

Remember you don't have to save the live video to your Instagram grid after if you don't want to. You can delete it and pretend it never happened, ready to try again.

If you have done a live video before and you feel confident with them, your challenge is to do another this week and look at how you can add them regularly into your content calendar.

Plan the next few lives in advance to keep you accountable. If you are looking for some content ideas, research posts on social media that you feel comfortable talking about in more detail and do a live on those.

Here are some suggestions for you:

o Show your products (no face needed but it's nice to see!)
o Share what you have coming up

o   Tell us about a new service or launch
o   Share a piece of valuable information or advice
o   Record a live video with someone else

Schedule your live videos in your calendar and give yourself a reward when they're done!

Day 60: Experiment with sharing reels

If you follow me on Instagram you might have noticed that I love a reel. An Instagram reel is a type of video you can share on Instagram that can be a variety of lengths but they are generally short, snappy content.

What is really interesting is that over the last few years of doing The Best 90 Days Ever membership, the advice for reels has changed so much.

While reels used to be all about pointing at text and dancing, I feel like they have changed a lot. Of course, if you still want to do some pointing and dancing who am I to stop you?

My reels have definitely changed from more of a production usually involving my dog's Halloween pumpkin costume, to simple videos and text that literally take me minutes to make.

Today's task is to look at the explore page of Instagram reels and see how you could replicate one of the videos that catches your attention.

If you watch someone giving a tip or hack – how could you share your own relevant tip? If you like aesthetic videos, how can you replicate them with your own content? If you hear any audios that you like, save them to use later, just click the name of the audio at the bottom and then the save tab at the top.

Write down any ideas for reels that you think you would be able to add to your content schedule over the next few weeks.

Some of the reels that are popular right now are:

o A general short video around 10 seconds long with some text over the top
o A video of you sharing a message or giving advice
o A video where you have recorded a voiceover

I love watching reels that have original content, which is why featuring you or your voice can help to build that connection with your audience.

Using the ideas you've written down, try a different type of reel today and see how you find it.

There are plenty of tutorials and reels on Instagram that share useful advice. Have some fun with this! Marketing is an experiment to see what works for you.

Day 61: Plan out video content for your pillars

Let's go right back to the week two and look at our content pillars. What did you decide they would be?

Your task for today is to plan out an idea for a piece of video content for each of your content pillars.

An educational video might be a tutorial you've created that explains a process your customers have asked you. It could be a live Q&A answering questions from your audience or a voiceover describing the work that you do behind the scenes.

An entertaining video could use a funny trending audio sharing a myth about your industry that you want to show isn't true. It could be some outtakes from your podcast or a mistake you've made this week.

Video content that sells could be an informative reel explaining each of your products and services or a live video letting people know the best ways to work with you this month.

The thing I like the best about video is that it can be varied, so if you feel like your content needs changing because it's all looking the same, video can help you mix it up and do things differently.

Take a look at those content pillars and see how video content will help you to make sure each one is included in your social media posts.

 Go back to your content pillars and plan a video for each one.

Day 62: Record a video that isn't work related

Today's task is a little bit of fun! I want you to record a video that has absolutely nothing to do with work.

As I mentioned before when I was talking about the TikTok challenge, part of getting better at video is just practising and recording lots of videos. But you don't have to stick to creating videos just for your business.

This week see if you can record videos about something you're interested in, what you're doing this weekend, a recipe you love to cook, a walk you've been on recently or a fun activity.

I love sharing videos about car boot sales or the bargains I've found at the charity shop. They help me to feel more confident about filming in public and improve my video skills.

There's no pressure to share this video (although if it's a video of your dog we definitely want to see it) but I do want to encourage you to be taking more videos.

Many of the reels I share are made up of random snippets of video I've taken without any pre-planning, so get used to filming and see what you can come up with!

Day 63: See how you can improve your videos

I hope you've enjoyed this week and it's helped you to start to get out of your comfort zone and explore different ways that you could be using video for your business.

For our final day of video content week I want to see how we can improve our videos going forward. This might be a challenging one today but it will be a good thing!

Today your task is to look at the videos you've taken and shared this week to see if you can find ways to improve them.

Watch your videos back and notice what you could change to make them better. I know it feels cringey but you might see that you always look away, the sound isn't great or the lighting could be improved.

You might find that your transitions need some work so using a template will make them easier or taking away your notes for a live video will stop you from looking down.

Watch the videos of creators you admire and think about what they do in their videos to make them more engaging and what's working well.

To finish off video week I thought I'd leave you with some of my top tips. I'm sure these will change over time but I hope you find these useful!

Here are a few tips for you when you're sharing reels or a TikTok:

o   Make sure all of your videos and images are portrait because that's the orientation of reels and TikTok, and they fill the screen so there is no blank space.
o   Use a trending audio to get a higher reach, look for the upwards arrow on songs when you are scrolling the reels page.
o   Save audios to use later by tapping the song and clicking save.

o Look on the explore page for inspiration and save the videos that catch your eye. Make notes about what's working in them.
o Always use captions on videos and stories so people can read them if they have their phone on silent. Use the caption sticker to add them to stories and reels.
o If you don't want to record videos, you can use images of your products or services.
o But it's also good to take lots of short videos each day. Whenever you're taking a picture, take a video too.
o Use the self-timer option if you're lip-syncing so you don't have to click record and jump back in the frame.
o Drag the videos at the sides to crop them when you're editing the video, shorter choppier videos keep people's attention.
o Make sure it's clear what your video is about on your profile grid with some text or a cover image.
o Wipe your phone camera before you record.
o Try to use the back camera as it will be better quality.
o Record videos in natural light or by a window.
o Create a theme or a video series that helps you to stay consistent.
o Have fun and try something new with your videos.

Week 9: Checklist

You might already be feeling confident about videos, in which case I hope this week has helped spark some new ideas to try something different.

If this was your first taste of video content, well done! I promise it gets easier, both with the technology side and with your confidence.

Video content is such a broad topic so use these tips and apply them to the platform that works the best for you and plays to your skill set. It isn't about who is the loudest or the most confident, you can have successful videos that don't show your face. But it is about using video content in a way that makes the most sense for you and your business.

Here's your checklist to tick off:

- ☐ Start documenting your day with videos
- ☐ Record a different type of video
- ☐ Film a live video or prepare for one
- ☐ Experiment with sharing reels
- ☐ Plan out video content for your pillars
- ☐ Record a video that isn't work related
- ☐ See how you can improve your videos

Week 10: Email marketing – Send emails that sell and grow your business

My business changed when I started email marketing. I know that probably sounds dramatic but it really did.

I can remember setting up my first newsletter on the train to Manchester, designing the header in my notebook and finally getting my audience signed up to receive 'The Social Sunday'.

From then I was able to email my growing list every single Sunday with marketing advice, offers and availability of my services. I loved sending those newsletters and it was only because I wanted more flexibility that I stopped sending them on a Sunday and started including the whole week.

Email marketing is a great way to build stronger connections with your audience and talk to them more personally than you might on social media.

It doesn't need to be intimidating or take a long time to set up either. Most platforms have a step-by-step guide and templates you can use to make the process much easier.

During this week I will use the words 'email marketing' and 'email newsletter' interchangeably. I know that some people like to differentiate between the two but my email newsletter contains both informative and promotional information so I use both phrases. For the time being, let's not make it complicated!

Day 64: Decide what your goal for this week will be

Welcome to email marketing week! I have been trying to think of an example of a small business that shouldn't be using emails in their marketing plan but I really can't think of any. Even if you're fully booked, emails can be a great way to start a waitlist for your services or promote the digital products you have.

The good news is if you're already writing social media posts you're halfway there with content. Emails can be adapted from the words you've already written to save time and be consistent with your messaging.

For today's task I want you to do the same as you did for video week and decide what your end goal for this week will be. Fill in the gap at the end of this sentence:

'By the end of this week I'm going to...'

There are lots of things you could do with emails so here are some suggestions:

o Research GDPR and get my email platform up and running
o Plan a way to get more subscribers
o Think of ways to increase clicks or replies on your emails
o Get started with email marketing
o Create something to sell in my emails
o Plan the next few emails in advance
o Make a new lead magnet

Depending on where you are in the world, the General Data Protection Regulation (GDPR) or UK GDPR is something that you might need to consider if you are starting an email list or collecting data in your business. I would recommend spending some time researching this before you begin so you can make sure that you are compliant from the very beginning.

If you don't have a newsletter yet, think about the ways you could set one up this week. If you do, how could you improve your content and grow your list?

 Finish the sentence: 'By the end of this week I'm going to…' and set a goal for your email marketing.

Day 65: Set up email templates

If you want to make email marketing easy, setting up templates is definitely the way to go.

I use a template for every email I send and duplicate the format each time. It means they look consistent, but it also saves me so much time. Setting up a template can take the decision making out of your email marketing so you know it follows the same structure for every email.

If you're just getting started with email marketing, pick a platform that you enjoy using and test out some of the free templates first. Before you commit to an email platform, make sure you find it easy to navigate and it's something you will actually use. We don't want to put anymore barriers in our way!

Most platforms will have templates you can use for your emails, your landing pages, forms and even promoting a special offer. These will vary depending on whether you are a product or service business so make sure that the template will help you to achieve your email marketing goals.

Your task for today is to look at where you could use templates on your emails to make things easier and start to set them up.

Browse through some of the available templates and have a go at adding in the logo, fonts and colours that you want to use for your email newsletters. If you already send a newsletter, you could test out creating a new landing page template to encourage more subscribers or even run a special email challenge (more about this later).

If you don't have your email set up yet, your task is to sign up for some free accounts and look at the options available. I have previously used Mailchimp and now I use Flodesk, but do your research and most importantly make sure it's a platform you can use easily and enjoy spending time on.

Day 66: What is the purpose of each of your emails?

This task was a little bit of tough love for one of our members who admitted to me that they didn't really have a plan or a purpose for their emails. So, guess what? Your task today is to remind yourself what the purpose of your emails is.

If you're just getting started you're in an even better position to plan ahead and decide what the purpose of your emails is going to be.

There are lots of possible reasons and your answers are likely to be different for each email you send, but it's important your emails really do cover the purpose you intended. If you want to connect and sell but spend 100% of the time connecting, where is the selling going to come from?

Some of your purposes might include:

o   Selling your products or services
o   Connecting with your audience
o   Promoting an event
o   Doing customer research
o   Increase your engagement

Now ask yourself honestly, is my newsletter doing that?

If you want to sell: Are you actually asking for the sale? Add some information about your latest product with a button so your subscribers can click through your email to buy it.

If you want to connect: Are you just telling people about yourself and not encouraging a response? Tell a story that people will relate to and want to reply with their own experiences.

If you want to do research: Are you making it as easy as possible for them to answer? Have you included a link to a Google form with some questions or added them into the email?

Your task today is to think about the purpose and create a plan for how you're going to make it clear in the email you're sending.

 Add your purpose to your workbook and plan your emails for the next few weeks.

Day 67: Plan a way to grow your email list

How are you getting on with your email marketing goals? Have you planned ways that you're going to get started or grow your list? Today's task will help!

The first area we're going to look at is growing your email list. If you're in the process of setting up your list, keep note of this page and come back to it when you're ready.

Growing my email list is always one of my goals and I've tried a few different things to get creative with it. One of my favourite ways was running a free 5-day email challenge called Social Media Sports Day. We had so much fun and it was really easy to do.

To grow your email list you might need to think of some unique ways to get people to want to hand over that email address.

Here are some ideas:

o Take part in an online event like a summit or bundle
o Hold a free workshop
o Run a free 3- or 5-day email challenge where you send daily emails
o Do a freebie swap with someone
o Share a post about your newsletter
o Host a competition
o Adding a sign up when customers buy
o Share the link to your email sign up page
o Post on your social media
o Use Pinterest to promote a lead magnet
o Add a sign up at the bottom of a blog post

The final one and possibly the most important… When was the last time you actually told people about your email list? We assume that our audience will know all about it but it's probably been a while since you last reminded them.

Jyoti is one of my one to one clients and a member of The Best 90 Days Ever online membership. She is a Menstrual Cycle Coach and Yoga Teacher at Jyoti Rani and set a goal at the beginning of the 3 months to grow her email list in a way that would feel enjoyable but also fit in with the rest of her business.

We made a plan to run a free 5-day email challenge that would help people create an at home retreat over the autumn season to feel grounded and at ease, with new practices in their self-care toolkit. I say 'we' but Jyoti took the idea and ran with it to create a beautiful landing page for subscribers to sign up. As I'm writing this she is half way to her sign up goal, adding new people to her list and re-engaging current subscribers with a brilliant week of emails that will also help to promote her coaching offer too. Amazing.

Today's task is to pick your plan of action for growing your email list but also share your newsletter sign up form TODAY!

Add a question box on Instagram so people can give you their email address and share your landing page on Facebook to encourage people to sign up.

Mention it in a video, post about it in a group and tell your audience. You could even create a template for your stories that makes it easy to share your sign-up page.

When you've done that, make a quick plan of what you're going to do to grow. If you've decided it's a webinar, pick a month and make a note of a few topics. If you want to do a freebie swap, write down people that might be interested. Plan ahead and make it happen.

Map out your idea for growing your email newsletter.

Day 68: Create a newsletter series

Today's task is to create a newsletter series. This is such a good way of keeping people engaged with your newsletter and it will help you make creating content easy for yourself too.

If you're getting bored of your newsletter and finding it hard to tell people about it, this is a good way to make it more exciting for you to talk about too.

A newsletter series is a series of newsletters that talk about the same topic or a similar theme.

The *Wandering Aimfully* newsletters do this really well, just search Wandering Aimfully to find them. For around 6 weeks each email will cover a different area of a topic and go into detail about each one. You can click to read the previous emails if you missed them.

Here are a few ideas for what a newsletter series could be for your business:

o   Four to six emails that cover one topic in different ways
o   A daily email series with tips on a certain theme
o   A block of emails before taking a pause

This can be great for a pre-launch because you can start to talk in more detail about that subject and mention your upcoming launch. I will often increase the number of emails I send while I'm launching a new offer, so this gives you more content and examples to talk about.

Think about the topics from your content plan and SEO week that you could cover in a newsletter series.

To make this even easier to promote you could give your series a name and its own brand. Why not create a landing page or some graphics for your series to help you share it?

If you don't have a newsletter yet but you think a series is something you would like to do, take a look at some of your social media posts and get some ideas for what your series could be about. You can also start to make a list of future topics too!

Day 69: Review your lead magnet and welcome series

Today I would like you to take a look at your lead magnet and welcome email or sequence.

Before we start, you don't need to have either of these. They are optional extras and at some points in my business I've had neither, either or both.

A lead magnet is something that could encourage someone to sign up for your newsletter. It's usually a freebie they would receive once they have entered their email address.

A welcome email is the first email that they would receive when they sign up and a sequence is a series of emails that would be automatically sent in a specific order once they join your email list.

If you don't have a lead magnet yet, start planning! What would help your audience and encourage them to sign up?

Here are some suggestions:

o   A quiz where the answers are in the welcome emails
o   A PDF
o   A webinar
o   A video sequence
o   An email sequence
o   A discount code
o   Free delivery for life
o   An email or Facebook challenge
o   An eBook
o   Private blogs or access to something special

Once they have signed up to your email list, you can set up a welcome email that they will automatically receive.

The welcome email is the first email someone will receive from you and it usually has the highest open rate too. Think about the key things you want someone to know about you and your business, especially if your lead magnet might have been the first time they've heard from you.

What does your welcome email say? How could you improve or maximize it? Make sure that it's relevant and up to date, they are very easy to set up and forget to look at for months or years.

If you haven't set up your email list yet, start drafting your welcome email. Sign up for a few emails and see the type of welcome email they send. What do you like and dislike?

The welcome email is a part of creating a newsletter that people often procrastinate on because they don't feel like they can send their first email before it's set up. Use this time to get it done and you can start sending that welcome email with your newsletter right from day one.

 Make a plan for what your lead magnet is going to be and how it will help your audience.

Day 70: Check your email sign up forms work

This is your final task for email week and I'm giving you an easy task because I know this week has been heavy going!

Today's task is to check your email sign up forms on your website. I know it sounds simple, but you'd be surprised how many don't work, lead to somewhere else or go to the wrong segment.

When you know it works, see if you can improve it. Is it enticing? Does it say the problem you're solving with your emails? Does it say how often you're going to send it? Where is it on your page?

While you're doing this, why not pop over to some other websites and sign up for their emails too for inspiration. We don't want to copy them, this is all about looking at what they do and why it works.

Think about businesses that are in a totally different industry to you. You never know who you're going to get inspiration from!

Sign up for the big ones – I really like the John Lewis email which is a department store here in the UK, especially for seasonal inspiration.

Sign up for the smaller ones – I love the Be More With Less email, it has a round up of interesting articles to read and always feels calm when you open it.

Sign up for other small business owners emails that you would like to work with in the future. There might be an opportunity to reply to one of their newsletters and start a conversation with them.

Look at what they are saying, how they are structuring their emails and how a version of this could work for you.

Week 10: Checklist

How have you found this week? Is there anything that has been challenging or interesting for you? Email marketing doesn't need to be complicated and you get to decide a structure for your emails that works for you.

I hope you've been able to achieve that goal we set for our email marketing at the start of the week! If you haven't, try to plan in some time over the next couple of days to get started on it. Your emails don't have to be perfect right away to start sending them, and it's likely you might only have a small list at the beginning which is a great opportunity to practice.

Here's your email marketing checklist for this week:

- ☐ Decide what your goal for this week will be
- ☐ Set up email templates
- ☐ What is the purpose of each of your emails?
- ☐ Plan a way to grow your email list
- ☐ Create a newsletter series
- ☐ Review your lead magnet and welcome series
- ☐ Check that your email sign up forms work

Week 11: Engagement week – Use your marketing to interact with your customers

Engagement is one of those marketing words that can mean different things to different people. I think of it as the ways your audience can interact with your content or to put it even simpler, how you can start a connection with them.

We all know that likes aren't everything when it comes to our marketing, but engagement on your content can be a sign that you're building relationships with your audience and posting the right thing. A comment is a great way to have a conversation, a share shows your content is resonating and a save means it's good enough for them to come back to later. It also helps your content to be seen by more people, which is a win win!

This week is all about increasing engagement on your posts but for the reason of connecting with your audience and making sure you're on the right track with your content, not just for the sake of it.

If you're ready to start engaging your customers, let's do this!

Day 71: Increase engagement on your email newsletters

This week we're kicking things off with engagement week. Over the course of this week we're going to be looking at ways you can increase interactions on different platforms and first up is email marketing.

Last week we did lots of work to get started on our email marketing and improve the emails that we send, but it can be really frustrating when you send out an email to your list and don't get any replies.

Today I have some suggestions for you to help you increase the number of replies, clicks and shares of your email newsletter which will hopefully help you to increase your number of subscribers too.

If you don't send emails yet, see if you can use any of these tips for different areas of your marketing instead.

Here are some suggestions to try. Set a timer and see how many of these you can work on in 10 minutes.

o   Use a subject line people want to open, engagement starts as soon as they receive the email. I like to write something cheeky which teases what is going to be in it. My aim is to get the reader to think 'what does that mean? I want to know more!'.

o   Ask questions and encourage people to reply. Share a story that your audience will relate to and respond to. Email marketing can feel much more private than social media, so you can have conversations and build relationships. It's lovely to have a chat with one of your subscribers over email, so try and think of some questions to encourage it.

o You can use buttons to give people access to things like free downloads and PDFs, but you can also use them as a voting system or a quiz. They are great if you want your subscribers to answer a question by choosing between multiple options or picking a winner. I asked my email subscribers to help me choose the cover for this book!

o Share relatable experiences and things that people will connect with. It doesn't have to be about work, I always find a mention of a car boot sale sparks lots of conversations, as does gardening and dogs.

o Share interesting and useful tips. One of the emails I love to get is Liz Mosley's income review pie chart because it's really fascinating. She shares a yearly email with a pie chart to show what percentage of her income come from different areas of her business.

o Use numbers or a list so people know what to expect, for example 'In this email I'll share my five tips for XYZ'.

I'm not suggesting that you do all of these for every email you send, but why not pick one for your next email newsletter and spend 10 minutes adding an interactive element?

Day 72: Increase engagement on your Instagram stories

Our second day for engagement week is about increasing engagement in your Instagram stories. Stories are a great way for you to build a personal connection and reach more people when you feel like your grid posts aren't being seen enough.

If you can encourage people to interact with your stories then they are more likely to see them again first when they open up the Instagram app.

We are all busy which means if you want to get people to stop and engage with your stories, you're going to have to make it worth their while.

Here are some suggestions to increase engagement (and hopefully views!) on your Instagram stories.

o Give people options of what they want to see more of. Asking your audience what they want to see puts the work and the effort on to them, but giving them options uses much less energy and is more likely to get a response.

o Use Instagram stickers such as polls and sliders but think about the things your followers will enjoy answering. Many people will respond to a sticker because they are happy to answer it and they also want to see the responses from other people. Click the 'sticker' option which looks like a square with a folded corner and smiley face at the top of your Instagram stories.

o Create interactive content. Talking stories that ask a question can be much more engaging that just a static image. Show something unusual that will spark conversations. If you think something is interesting then it's likely someone else will, but often it's the everyday things that get people talking because we have a shared experience of them.

o Turn your Instagram stories into a game. Gamification is a popular word at the moment and because marketing doesn't feel easy for everyone, making it a game can be a good way to get engagement. Use polls and ask your audience to vote for different images, test their knowledge with a slider or do a pub quiz in your stories.

o Use the close friends feature to share specific content to a segment of your audience. You can use this to share personal content or even host fun challenges and activities for a part of your audience.

o Show your personality in your stories and talk about the things you are interested in. This is a great way to connect with your audience in more than just a surface level business way. When I shared about growing the flowers for our wedding or getting a bargain at the car boot sale, more people replied than with any business stories.

o Talking about growing flowers… ask questions that encourage your audience to help you, but they don't have to be related to work. 'What's the best way to grow seeds in a greenhouse?' would get me talking and whenever I have asked for gardening advice people have been quick to jump in and help which is lovely.

o I read an article the other day that said these are some of the things you can ask customers about – their needs, situations, experiences, desires or thoughts. Which one would make a good Instagram story for today?

Pick one of these to try and see how you get on. Try not to overthink it, remember Instagram stories only last for 24 hours and it's trial and error to get them right. Have some fun and experiment.

Day 73: Increase engagement on your grid posts

Today is about getting more engagement on your Instagram grid posts with some tips which can also be used for other platforms like Facebook and LinkedIn.

Your task for today is to spend 10 minutes on each of these areas over this week and experiment with what works.

If you want to increase engagement, you need to research what's working. Social media changes all the time and a little bit of extra knowledge means you are more likely to get your content seen by your audience. That doesn't mean that you need to spend hours scrolling your competitors or comparing yourself to viral posts, but if you are going to put some time and effort into your content, you might as well give it the best chance to be seen.

Take a look on your Instagram explore page and see what's catching your eye. Is it informative carousel posts? Personal images and honest captions? Funny memes?

There are a few different types of engagement we're looking for with grid posts and these are also known as a call to action. A call to action is there to show or tell the reader what action they should take after they have read that post. For our Instagram grid posts we're going to look at likes, comments, shares, saves and a click through.

Likes: Often images with a person or living thing (like a dog or plant) do best for likes. When was the last time you shared something personal? Maybe you could write a post about an experience you've had recently or how you feel in your business. You could celebrate a win or share something that hasn't gone to plan. Pop your face on your grid and see what happens!

Comments: If you want more comments, you need to give people something to reply to. Ask questions that people genuinely want to answer, give them multiple options or turn it into a game. Ask your audience to help you choose something in your business or add to the post 'tell me something below about XYZ'.

Shares: Shares are tricky because people will share posts for different reasons, but generally they share something useful or entertaining. Think about the type of content your audience would enjoy and want to share with their audience too. Memes and quotes work well for shares but it does need to fit with your brand.

Saves: Saves usually happen when there is information people want to come back to (or copy, but we'll ignore that!). Creating useful graphics is a good way to do this. They might take a little longer but spend some time thinking of ways you could create an informative carousel graphic with up to ten slides. Use this as a template for future posts too.

Clicks: Finally, sometimes we want people to click through to our website instead! Make it easy by keeping your bio links updated, adding links to your Instagram stories or asking people to comment on your post so you can direct message (DM) them with your website.

Online member Helen Jane Campbell is a coach for Founders, Freelancers and Rebels. She took part in engagement week and looked into the different types of posts that were working for her account. I received the best Instagram message from her to say that over the last 90 days her engagement was up with +21.5% more accounts reached, +41.7% accounts engaged and +3.3% more followers. That engagement is impressive!

Helen also sent me this lovely email with feedback on The Best 90 Days Ever:

> *As someone who ran marketing teams and PR teams at a high level for big-name clients I have to be honest... I NEVER usually sign up for marketing groups or courses. Why? I always assume my 20+ years experience and qualifications will be enough. But clearly that's not true. BECAUSE I am learning something every single day from you. And I'm so, so happy about this!*

Your task for today is to focus on one of these areas each day for the next few days. Look at the content you've posted recently and be honest about whether it has a focus to achieve one of these goals. Not everything needs to have an aim, but if you want more engagement it's good to pick an area you would like to improve. Challenge yourself!

Day 74: Increase engagement on your video content

Today is about increasing engagement on your video content. Video content is a great way to show your personality and explain more about your products and services, which means it's even better when we can encourage people to comment on or share those videos.

Today's task is to pick one of these 10-minute marketing tips and include it in your next video.

These suggestions can be used for different types of video content, whether it's Instagram stories, lives, reels and TikTok or even Zoom calls. Which one will you use first?

o   Show your personality. The videos that feel like they consistently do the best over time are the ones that feature your face or include a voiceover. How could you bring some personality into your next video?

o   Take a look at reels or TikTok to get some inspiration for different types of video content. See which ones are getting lots of views or sparking conversations and look for accounts that offer advice about how to grow on that platform. They will often be ahead of the game when it comes to trends and if you follow their advice you are more likely to grow quickly.

o   Remember to think about the platform you're using. I would go to reels and TikTok for something quick and easy to understand and YouTube for longer pieces of content. For shorter videos, keep to the point you're making and tell them what the call to action is (the thing you want them to do after they have watched the video).

o   Just like you would in a post, ask questions! If you're doing a live or a story, ask questions for people to reply to either by DM or in the comments. This is great if you're nervous about doing a live and forgetting what to say as having a question to answer in the comments can give you more direction.

o   Use the tools within the apps. Most apps now have options to include engagement in your videos. We've already mentioned stickers in stories, but think about how you can include a poll in your reels, filters on TikTok or quizzes and polls on Zoom.

o   Have a hook right away. Think about what will capture their attention so they want to stop scrolling and stay and watch the whole video.

o   Try collaborating with someone else on a video. This could be by doing a live video or a joint reel that you can add them as a collaborator to. This can be a great way to increase engagement especially if you know you both bounce off each other. Pick a topic to discuss and get the audience to participate with questions too.

o   Remember our grid post options from Day 73. Does your video make people want to share or save it? Have you included something useful or funny?

Take a look back at some of your most popular videos and think about why they have worked for your audience. See if you can take elements of them forward into your next videos too.

Day 75: Increase your own engagement

Today's task is about looking at your own engagement. The more engagement you put in, the more engagement you are likely to receive, so if you want to get some engagement back, it's a good idea to start being generous in giving some out.

This helps you to connect with your audience and have a better connection. But it also helps your account grow because as people are scrolling they will see your name in comments on lots of different pages. I see a lot of people talk negatively about doing this as a way of growing your account, and I do think if it's done the wrong way it can make your page seem like a bot.

Social media is meant to be social and building relationships goes two ways. If we want to start getting more comments, likes and shares, we have to be honest with how much we are doing that for others. Plus, how great does it feel when someone leaves you a comment with a compliment on your post? Why wouldn't you want to give that great feeling to someone else?

Today's task is to pick some of these engagement activities and see how many you can do throughout the day in just 10 minutes.

Try to do them when you have spare time or you would usually turn to scrolling, like when the kettle is boiling or you're waiting in a queue.

If you *really* want to challenge yourself, every time you pick up the phone unnecessarily to scroll or go on social media, do one of these instead:

o   Reply to a story
o   Answer a question on a poll
o   Comment on a post (any platform)
o   Comment on a blog or article
o   Share a story about another business
o   Watch a live video and ask a question
o   Reply to a reel or TikTok
o   Reply to an email newsletter
o   Leave a review or testimonial

I hope that doing this will also show you how many posts make it very difficult to engage with them because they have no questions to reply to! Try to make sure yours don't do the same.

As you're doing this look for some good examples that you can take inspiration from and make a note of what they do well. It's likely you'll start to see some familiar names popping up frequently so look at what they're doing and see how you can follow the same pattern.

Day 76: Increase your client engagement

Today's engagement task is one that needs a little bit more time, but your task is just to make a plan in 10 minutes. This is all about client engagement which could be before, during and after working together.

Surveys: You can use surveys at different points in your client journey, but one you might not have thought about is a 'why didn't you buy' survey. This can be great to find out their thoughts after a launch and use their feedback to improve for next time.

User Generated Content (UGC): UGC is a good way to engage more with your clients or customers after you've worked together. Ask your audience to share photos and videos with you that you can use for testimonials and you can even give them a reward to say thank you.

Giveaways: Grow your audience or reward your current customers with giveaways. I like these for current customers as I think they re-engage people and get everyone excited again! You can do these in your private group, email list or even on your podcast.

Sharing progress: Think about ways you can engage with your clients *during* the process of working with you. We have a habit tracker for The Best 90 Days Ever group but it could be a monthly scheduled meeting, a platform where you could check in with your client progress or a timeline to show where you're at in a project.

Feedback and testimonials: Once you've finished working together it's great to get feedback and testimonials. You can do this with a Google form, Dubsado or even sending an email. I also use these forms before I start working with a client to have details to check in with during the process.

If there are areas of your client process that you would like more engagement, think about ways you could improve them. Make a plan to add them into your next client relationship and see how it impacts the way you work together.

Day 77: Increase engagement with surveys and quizzes

Our final day of engagement week! I know this has been quite a full week but remember you can always come back to these tasks, this book is designed to be picked up again and again.

Today's task is about surveys and quizzes. There are so many different ways you can use them for your business to find out more about your audience and make sure that you're giving them what they are looking and asking for.

Pick one of these and make a plan for how you would add it into your current marketing plan.

Pre-launch survey: Before you launch a new offer, get some feedback from your audience. Creating a survey with open ended questions (not just yes or no) is a good way to take some of the language your audience is using and add it to your content. Be clear on who you want to answer, whether it's a type of person or specific experiences they have had. You can do this with a simple Google form and even just four or five responses is really useful.

Quiz lead magnet: Quizzes have become quite popular as a lead magnet recently. You could create a quiz so your audience can find out what type of 'person' they are and offer them specific advice. It's also useful for finding out more information about your audience. If a quiz is enjoyable to take part in, people are more likely to share them.

Games for your marketing: Things like a flow chart, a personality quiz (if you picked mostly Bs, etc) and even just simple questions.

I saw this saying the other day which I really liked.

> *Consumers have plenty of things to say – you simply have to know what to ask.*
>
> Colton Gardner

Today's task is to give yourself 10 minutes to think about where you would like to get more information from your audience and how you can introduce a quiz to help with that.

Week 11: Checklist

How do you feel about engagement after this week? It can be really easy to get into a routine where we just put content out for the sake of it and forget about the purpose.

Social media is a great place to connect with other business owners, have interesting conversations and learn more about them. But to do that we have to reach out and find those people we want to have conversations with!

Hopefully this week will help you to increase your interactions going forward and create some great relationships too.

- ☐ Increase engagement on your email newsletters
- ☐ Increase engagement on your Instagram stories
- ☐ Increase engagement on your Instagram grid posts
- ☐ Increase engagement on your video content
- ☐ Increase your own engagement
- ☐ Increase your client engagement
- ☐ Increase engagement with surveys and quizzes

Week 12: Launching – Create a plan to launch new offers

This is our penultimate week and I've saved one of the worst until last. Just kidding! This is actually one of my favourite weeks and it's had some great results for our online members.

Launching can feel scary to many business owners because it's often seen as promoting a huge project that needs months to prepare and all of your time and your energy.

When I think about launching, I think about shouting a little bit louder about a particular offer or part of my business for a period of time. It can be a free challenge I'm doing, a paid digital product or even The Best 90 Days Ever. Your launch can be one day long or it can be 3 months long, it's about what works for you.

Hopefully this week will show you that launching is nothing to be worried about and can actually be fun!

Day 78: Look at your current offers and decide any gaps to fill

Welcome to launch week! This week is all about the steps you can take when you're launching something new or relaunching something you've promoted before.

This could be a course, a service, a product, a newsletter, a workshop or even a free challenge. You can celebrate so many things with a launch and it's great for content too. Don't be intimidated by launching, this is all about creating a launch plan that's right for you.

This week is about planning ahead and making things as simple and easy as possible. I've seen launching be made really over complicated so we just want to decide *the thing* and then tell people about *the thing*!

Today's task is to look at all of your current offers. Are there any gaps that you want to fill? It could be that you don't have any low-cost offers or group services. It might be that you are a product business and don't have a way to encourage repeat customers. You might decide you need a digital product or something pre-recorded that people can buy at any time.

I know there are some people who will tell you that you must have a free and low-cost offer and you must have an expensive option too, but there is no one-size-fits-all for business. Decide what business plan you want to have.

When you've done that, write down all the different people you help, everything you have knowledge about and all the things that people have asked you for in the past.

When you have your list of topics that could become a new offer, start to mind map the format that offer might take. It could be a course, an eBook, a one-to-one service, but you might find that once you've written it down it becomes obvious what it should be.

One of our members did this task and realized there was a gap in their offers for a short DIY class. They decide to teach some of the tools they were sharing in their one-to-one sessions but as a group workshop and guess what? People signed up!

Pick something to use as an example for this week so we can get straight into the logistics of a launch and you have an idea to use as a good practice run. It could be a new offer, something you haven't spoken about in a while, your newsletter, a product, a free challenge or even a podcast.

Think about the time you have left for this quarter. What can you realistically do in that time? Let's get ready to launch it.

 Use the prompts to write down a list of topics you could create an offer about.

Day 79: Plan out the logistics of your launch

Today's task is to look at the logistics of your launch. It's best to do this early on so you can see how much work is needed.

Start by picking a launch date. Think about the hours you have available and the time that would work best for your customers. Don't choose a week that's going to be stressful for you or a day when other things are likely to come up.

Do you want to avoid the summer months because people are away or is your offer perfect for that season? Are you taking December off so it wouldn't be a good idea to put anything in your diary for then? Is the start of the year when people would be thinking about what you're offering?

I usually avoid half term and bank holidays if it's an online event because people end up having other plans. Pick a date that works for you so you can give it your full attention.

Then work backwards and decide how long you're going to launch for. With The Best 90 Days Ever online membership I start talking about it for around 6 weeks before and then I have a 2 week launch where I share daily(ish!) content to promote it.

Two weeks is a long time and I only do this because most of it is pre-written. Your launch can be 1 week or even a few days as a flash offer. Think about what works for you.

Now you know how long it will be, how much content do you need? I like to decide a maximum and a minimum for my launch content.

The maximum is the amount I would share if I was feeling really good. I had time to plan ahead and I was focused and excited about the launch.

The minimum is the lowest amount I would be able to share to make this launch successful. This could be the same as the normal amount of content I would post but with a specific focus on the launch product.

You can use this to work out how much content you need to create. If you want to send four newsletters, share 16 posts and eight reels, that gives you something to aim for. Use this to create your marketing plan ready for your launch.

 Pick a launch date and decide how much content you need to create.

Day 80: Get all of your launch ideas down on paper

The next step that works for me when it comes to launching is to get all of the ideas out of my head and onto a big piece of paper.

When I know roughly how much content I need to create, I use my Easy Launching with Trello template which you can find on my website www.hicommunications.co.uk and start to fill it in.

The best way I've found to do this is to mind map everything I want to talk about during the launch and everything I might already have to promote it.

Try and think about general elements of the product or service and then narrow it down to specific topics that your audience will be thinking about and searching for right now.

How can you make it fun or different? How can it be even more interesting or exciting for your audience? What is going to be a focus for your audience over the next few months? What are the main words, themes or outcomes that come up for you?

This doesn't need to be perfect, I usually use a scrap of paper and remember you don't need to use all of the ideas. I often find it helpful to talk to someone else about this too and see what they think.

When you're done, take a look at that piece of paper and start adding some of the main areas to a Trello board or the place you store your content.

I have a board for each quarterly launch of *The Best 90 Days Ever* so I can come back to that content and reuse it depending on the season. This saves so much time and it means you don't have to start from scratch every time you want to launch.

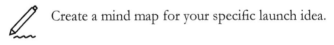 Create a mind map for your specific launch idea.

Day 81: Who, what, where, when, why?

Today's task is something you can do for everything you launch and even each time you write a post or a blog post. It's a good way to make sure you have your target audience in mind every time you're creating content.

Set a timer for 10 minutes and think about your launch offer.

Who: Who is it for? Who would buy it? Who wouldn't buy it? Who do you picture in your mind when you're talking about this offer?

What: What actually is it? What do you get? What does it do? What are the benefits or the outcomes? Explain it in very simple terms and don't expect everyone to know what is included. This could be the first time they have ever heard about it so make it clear.

Where: Where does it take place? Where can they buy it? Where would they use it? Is this product or service available for anyone anywhere in the world?

When: When does it start or end? When would someone need this? When wouldn't they need it? When do calls or sessions take place during it if you have them?

Why: Why would they want or need it? Why are you the best person to be offering this? Why wouldn't they want it? Why are you running it now?

You can also ask yourself what their objections would be. Why might they not want or need it now? What might stop them from wanting to buy it if they aren't sure?

You don't need to convince people that they should buy your offer, but these could be simple objections that are easy for you to fix or resolve that you hadn't thought of. It's great feedback and can give you ways to improve.

Use these answers to think about your ideal client while you're writing content. I like to create a template for a post that answers all of these questions every time I do a launch and it's always one of the best for sales.

 Write down your who, what, where, when, why.

Day 82: Look at content you can reuse for your launch

Today's task is to look at the content you already have that will make this launch even easier. I bet that you have a bank of content that could be reused and chopped up to save you time and keep a consistent message.

If you created lots of content back in batch creating week, there is a good chance that some of that content could be used for your launch.

Today's task is to go on a treasure hunt and look for all that reusable content. See if you can find:

Content that you can use for the offer itself: This could be as simple as a suggestion from a member of your audience that sparks an idea for a new course or a lead magnet.

But it could also be videos, a PDF or eBook or even information that you have previously shared in a workshop. The key to remember is, don't start from scratch if you have already spoken about this topic before.

Content you can use for social media: Start scrolling back through your social media and see if you've covered any relevant or similar topics before. This could be in posts, reels or even live videos. You could reuse some of your favourite images or copy the captions into your Trello board to adapt and come back to later.

Content you can use for emails: This could also be social media content, but it might include emails you've sent before or blog posts that can be adapted into a newsletter. If you have the energy you could create a short email series in the lead up to the launch that talks about a topic to help you promote your offer.

When you've done your mind map you will hopefully notice there are certain themes you may have spoken about before. If you haven't spoken about the topic before, I would ask yourself honestly if it really fits in with the rest of your content plan. If you've never spoken about it or something similar, is it a random offer that is based on a trend and not part of your marketing strategy?

Louise Willington owns Freestyle – Professional and Creative Hair Design, a hair salon in Pontypridd, South Wales. She is an online member and took part in our launching week challenge to promote her new hair extensions service at the salon.

Here's what she had to say about launching week:

> *This week has definitely kicked me up the butt to get a better plan and structure to my launch, what I thought was a launch routine certainly wasn't. This week alone I have come up with the name of the launch for my extensions range, designed the templates in Canva, branded them and planned the date for my pre-launch and my launch.*
>
> *I've started to write the headlines for the posts and I've taken some new pictures and reused some old ones. I've briefly written pointers for my blog, which I will reuse for the newsletter, I love the recycling of content ideas. All that in just 6 days. I literally set my timer for 15 minutes a day and it's surprising what you can achieve. I've not finished it but now I'm just adding to it all rather than starting from scratch. I love The Best 90 Days Ever, it's been a blast and it's not over yet.*

Collect all the content you can find and store it somewhere for this launch. I find it so much easier to write content when I'm not starting from scratch, and you'll be surprised how many things can be adapted and reused to save you time.

Day 83: Plan your launch visuals

When you're planning a launch, you also want to think about the visuals that you will need. This is where you can have some fun!

Of course, you don't need to make anything extra to promote your new offer if you don't want to. But having a name, logo and some graphics can make it much easier to talk about.

Today's task is to think about any visuals you'd like to include for your launch and start to create them. Here are some examples:

A name: Giving your product or service an exciting name makes it so much easier to talk about and much more memorable for your audience. Coming up with a name is one of my favourite parts of a launch plan. You can bring your followers along from the beginning and ask them to help you choose it.

Some of the things that help me come up with a name include alliteration, thinking about the current season and linking it to other products or services I already have. Go on a walk and see if you can come up with some ideas. If I didn't love the name 'The Best 90 Days Ever' so much it would be much harder to promote!

A logo and graphics: If you have a great name for your new product and service why not speak to a graphic designer to create a logo and some graphics you could use for your launch? I am very lucky that my husband Tom creates these for me when I'm launching, but if he wasn't able to, it is something I would still invest in for my business and outsource.

You might want to think about setting up some simple templates that you can use to share information like the 'who, what, where, when' post we discussed earlier and reuse it for future launches. Think about if you need separate graphics for your affiliates too, it's always good to plan ahead.

Images: Having some images related to your launch will make creating social media posts much easier. If you have a theme, think about how you could use props to keep your imagery consistent. My favourite launch has been for Social Media Sports Day, a free email challenge we planned. We had the egg and spoon race, sack race, a whistle and sweat bands which made taking photos for social media much more fun and relevant.

Images can make your offer really recognizable and people will often need reminding a few times that they haven't signed up yet, I know I do! Having clear images says 'are you joining us?' without even having to say it.

Video: While you're there, why not get some video content too? Take snippets for reels, videos of you explaining what the offer is and even a plan for live videos will all help to promote your launch.

Video can be great for your launch plan because you can properly explain what it's going to include without being limited to a graphic or a word count. I love a live video because it takes the time that it takes. If you only have 10 minutes, go live and chat for 10 minutes about your offer.

The right visuals can help you to reach your high goals when it comes to your launch, so have a play around with what that's going to look like for you and plan ahead to make them part of your content plan.

Day 84: Set goals for your launch

The final task for launch week is to set goals. When you're planning a launch, set yourself a low and a high goal, if there is quite a big gap between them you could also set a middle goal too.

The low goal is something you're pretty confident you'll reach but you would still feel happy with that result. It can take the pressure off your launch because once you've reached it, anything else feels like a bonus.

The high goal is a number that you think, wow that would be amazing! It's still realistic but would feel incredible to achieve. The great thing about a high goal is that it encourages you to keep going and push a little bit more. If you were only a few people away from your high goal, you could have some surprise back-up content that you pull out of the bag. The high goal has been really motivating for me on my launches. I don't achieve it every time, but when I do, it really does feel amazing and there is a certain energy going into that round of *The Best 90 Days Ever*.

Your goals could be to host an event and have a certain number of people buy tickets, you could run a newsletter challenge and count the new subscribers or you could count the sales of a product launch.

I like to celebrate every single person that comes into my launches! I've seen people do some really cool things to show who has signed up, like writing their names on the wall or sending them a personalized video. What would feel like a fun way for you to celebrate them?

Set a high goal and a low goal for your launch.

Week 12: Checklist

How do you feel at the end of launch week? I hope this week has shown that launching can be a really fun thing to do in your business and it's all about what you want your launch to be.

Launching is about bringing all of the parts of your marketing together to talk about one specific product, service or offer. It helps to give you that focus and consistency I know so many of us are looking for. Whatever the outcome of your launch, you'll be more visible and show up for your business during that time.

I like to plan out my launches on a big wall calendar at the start of the year, but you don't need to wait until January. Whenever you're picking up this book is a good time to plan your next launch!

Good luck, I can't wait to see you reach your maximum goal!

Tick off this launching checklist as you go.

- ☐ Look at your current offers and decide any gaps to fill
- ☐ Plan out the logistics of your launch
- ☐ Get all of your launch ideas down on paper
- ☐ Who, what, where, when, why?

☐ Look at content you can reuse for your launch
☐ Plan your launch visuals
☐ Set goals for your launch

Month 3: Check in – Almost there!

We are so close to the end now, our final week is right around the corner.

Hopefully by now these 10-minute marketing prompts are starting to become part of your routine. If you can work on your business for just 10 minutes each day you'll really start to see progress and your mindset around your marketing will change too.

Marketing doesn't have to be a chore, it can be something fun and enjoyable that helps you to get results. Keep checking in with those goals and look at the progress you're making with your marketing.

Here are some questions to ask yourself before we go into our final week.

Is there anything I would be disappointed I haven't achieved over the last 3 months that I could focus on next week?
If there is still something on your list that you really hoped you would have time to work on, now is a great opportunity to put it as your top priority and make some space for it next week. Although these 90 days give you suggestions for prompts to do each day, if you know there is something you should be working on please make that the priority for you!

Which habits would I like to continue with after these 90 days?
Some of the tasks in this book will appeal more to you than others, which is a good thing! Look at the tasks you really enjoyed and see how you can make them part of your marketing routine each week.

Which habits would you like to stop after these 90 days?
When we're adding new habits to our routine it often means we need to remove some of the old habits that we no longer need. See if there's anything that comes up for you that's taking up your valuable time when you could be moving forward on other projects. Scrolling on my phone is a big habit for me that I always want to stop.

Final week

Week 13: Sales – How to use everything we've learnt to make more sales

It's our final week! This is a slightly shorter week because I named this *The Best 90 Days Ever* and not *The Best 91 Days Ever*, but I think I've saved the best till last.

This week is sales week, and my goal is for every reader to make back at least the cost of this book with these prompts, but if you go on to be millionaires then that's even better.

Some small business owners feel uncomfortable about selling. It can be difficult to feel confident about what you do and promote the ways that people can buy from you. But the reality is that this is a business and not a hobby, for it to be sustainable it has to make money.

Selling doesn't need to be uncomfortable at all.

Let's finish these 90 days on a high and really focus on sales week!

Day 85: Set yourself an income challenge

This week is all about selling. I hope these tasks will help you to increase sales for your business and feel confident about selling your products and services.

You have two tasks for today. The first is to set yourself a goal for this week, something that feels achievable but exciting. It could be a financial goal to make a certain income number or it could be to sell X number of a product or spaces on a course.

In the group we play a game of good, better, best. We'll have a number, let's use 9 for this example, and we'll try and make the good, better, best of that amount for the week. The aim is that it's a fun challenge to help you reach the next income goal and because it's a number set by someone else, it doesn't matter too much which amount you finish on!

It could be:

£9
£90
£900
Or £9000

Pick your option and let's make a plan to achieve it.

Sioned is a Digital Illustrator and GIF Designer and the founder of Mwydro. She always takes on the sales week challenges and smashes them, so I thought I'd ask her what she thinks about them. Here's what she said:

> *I love the creativity and energy that comes with Sales Week. Like many others I can share a lot of content on social media, but often forget to actually push on the selling aspect of things. It was great to have that drive to push the sale of my services and products and to build my confidence in asking for the sale and chasing after leads. The last time I took part in Sales Week I made an additional £800 of sales that week!*

The second task for today is to do one thing that moves you closer to a sale. You probably already know what you need to do. **That thing you've been putting off.**

Could you offer a special discount? Send out an email? Put up a post with your products or services? Contact someone who was interested in your service and then went quiet?

There is usually something in the back of our minds that we know we aren't doing. Be brave and get it done today, we are all cheering for you!

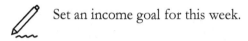 Set an income goal for this week.

Day 86: Make a list of all your products and services

Today's task is to do an inventory of everything you have to sell. When was the last time you went through and checked all your products and services?

These could include:

o   Physical products
o   Digital products
o   Products that are half finished
o   One-to-one and group offers
o   Things that you have done and could sell in the future (workshops, etc)
o   Ideas for future things to sell
o   Freebies that could be turned into offers

Write down how much everything sells for and see where you can find any gaps. You probably have so many potential things to sell waiting for you to get going on them!

Think about the journey people will take when they buy from you. We spoke about this briefly in week 12, launching week, and there is no one size fits all. But you might already have something ready and waiting to go that you haven't launched yet which fills an income gap.

Having multiple offers and products means people can work with you and buy from you wherever they are in their business journey.

Michelle Morgan Davies is a Journalist and PR expert at Have Your Say Stories. She is an online member and used sales week to give her business a boost. Here's what she said about our sales tasks:

> *The Best 90 Days Ever tasks have given me actionable strategies and inspiration to create offers and promote them with ease. When I came up with a webinar offering during Sales Week, Hannah helped me to choose a platform that would make everything simple. I made £100 from that online workshop. I also pushed myself to promote my power hour and look over old journalism pitches to see if anything could be reworked into a new story. I made £600 in total with the support of Hannah cheering me on.*

When you've done your inventory, look at the last time you promoted these offers. Is it an embarrassingly long amount of time? If it is, maybe it's no surprise that people aren't making a purchase from you. They don't know what you do!

Give yourself some time today to put it all down and look at where you think the gaps are in your offers and in your promotion. If you're feeling brave, why don't you write a post about that product you haven't spoken about in a while? Go on, I dare you!

Take an inventory of all your current products and offers.

Day 87: Write down who your offers help and reach out to them

This week is all about taking action. I always find that when I'm proactive, moving forward and feeling excited that good things happen!

Today's tasks are some journaling prompts for you to write down and explore. You can turn these answers into content too so you might find it easier to answer them digitally.

1 – Write a list of the problems that your products or services solve.

2 – If people spoke about your business, what would they say you offer?

3 – Write a list of the people who could, or have been, interested in your product or service and reach out to them.

It might not be to sell, it could be an email after a purchase, a newsletter or just a check-in to say hello. See if there's any feedback on your product or service and any additional help they need.

They might be previous customers, people who have messaged you, newsletter subscribers or even followers on Instagram. This is great for finding those enquiries you have forgotten about.

Keep this in mind if you're launching and have people who you think your 'thing' would be perfect for. You can reach out to them or think about them and their needs as you're writing your posts.

How many people are on your list that you could say hi to?

 Write a list of problems that your products and services solve.

Day 88: Pick from the list of 20 sales tasks

Today is all about trying something new to move you closer to a sale. I know that we are all at different stages of our businesses and what we have to sell so please adapt these tasks in a way that feels good for you.

I've created a list of 20 things you could do to move closer to a sale today and your task is to decide how many of the 20 you're going to aim for, then get started.

Remember this is all about 10-minute marketing tasks so try and make this quick and simple without overthinking them.

1. Do a live video talking about a product or service you offer
2. Hold a flash sale on some stock you want to clear
3. Send an email newsletter telling people a product or service and how they can buy it
4. Contact someone who was interested in your offer but went quiet
5. Mind map a new low-cost offer that doesn't take much energy for you
6. Contact people who have previously purchased and see if they need any more help
7. Create a bundle with offers together
8. Do a step-by-step guide of how an offer works
9. Look into other income streams like affiliates, brand ambassadors or courses
10. Tell us exactly who your product or service is for
11. Find a Facebook group where you can share your offer
12. Tell your audience five reasons why your offer is great
13. Look at something you have already created that you could sell or use as a lead magnet
14. Edit your website. Does the wording need tweaking? Would it encourage people to buy?
15. Tell us about your business on Instagram stories as if no one has ever heard about it before
16. Send a message or email to someone who you think would be interested in your offer
17. Write a 'who, what, why, when, how' post
18. Check the link in your bio and update it if you need to
19. Offer a discount when people sign up to your email or a workshop
20. Get the sales juices flowing and sell something around the house!

Try something new to promote your business that you haven't tried before. Get out of your comfort zone this week!

Day 89: Tell us your favourite product or service

Tell us what your favourite product or service is this month or ask the members of your team or audience to pick theirs and tell us why.

Your audience wants to know why these things are great. You created it, why do you think it's brilliant and people should buy it?

What have other people said about it? Share some lovely reviews or testimonials and show that other people love your offers too. They are a brilliant way to build trust and show your audience how that product or service has helped or been received by someone else.

Write a love note to your offer about why it's so brilliant and the different parts of it that you think are useful. We don't brag enough as business owners about how great our things really are. I know you've worked hard on your products and services, don't shy away from talking about them.

You can make this into a post, newsletter or blog, but it's a really great way to get more specific about something you sell.

Include some interesting facts about it, feedback from previous customers, details about cost, how it works, where they can buy it and why you love it.

Once you've done that, ask for a new testimonial too. Has someone bought from you recently? Would they be happy to leave you a review? Check in with your recent customers and ask them.

Make this part of your monthly routine so you can keep collecting new testimonials and reviews to share.

Day 90: Write a post on how people can work with you

Our final task for *The Best 90 Days Ever* might seem obvious, but you'll be surprised how many people forget to do this, myself included.

Your task for today is to write a post or an email to say all the ways someone can work with or buy from you right now.

It could have a list of your services, your top products, a discount offer or a deal you are running at the moment.

Now think about how you want to finish this post, what is your call to action? Have a look at every call to action you've been using and think about whether they are leading towards a sale. Have you told people how they can buy from you?

Make this into a template that you can adapt and share quarterly or every couple of months. It's a great reminder from your audience of how to work with you and it also helps if you often get enquiries about your availability.

Go and get those sales! Do this across all of your content including your posts, emails and videos but also look at your website too. Does it make people want to buy your product or book your service?

Week 13: Checklist

There we have it. Our final task of *The Best 90 Days Ever*. I hope this week has helped you to feel more confident about selling in your business.

It's so important that small business owners share what they do and feel proud about their products and services. You work so hard on your offers and you deserve to be paid for them too!

Here is our checklist for the final week of *The Best 90 Days Ever*:

- ☐ Set yourself an income challenge
- ☐ Make a list of all your products and services
- ☐ Write down who your offers help and reach out
- ☐ Pick from the list of 20 sales tasks

☐ Tell us your favourite product or service
☐ Write a post on how people can work with you

90 day check in: How have you found the last 90 days?

We made it! Wow it feels strange to see all 90 of these tasks written down. I hope you've enjoyed this book and had *The Best 90 Days Ever* in your business.

Have a little pause and when you're ready, come back and answer these questions.

What was your favourite week or task?

Is there a week that really stands out for you that has made a big impact in your business or sparked an idea? Remember you can keep coming back to these tasks and each time you might think of something new or different to add.

Which week or task did you find the most challenging?

There is always a week that we find difficult, graphic design is mine which is why I asked Liz to do it! Think about the reasons you found that week difficult and if it's because you need to outsource something in your business or learn more about a skill.

Are there any tasks you have bookmarked to come back to?

Although this book is full of 10-minute marketing tasks, there are plenty in here which you could spend much longer on if you wanted to. If there are tasks you have bookmarked to come back to, why not make a list of them so you can find them easily?

Conclusion

Well done for completing *The Best 90 Days Ever*! I really hope you have enjoyed the last 90 days working on your business and this becomes a book that you can keep turning to for marketing advice again and again.

The Best 90 Days Ever was something I created because I realized I needed it just as much as the members did. A reminder each day to help you be more consistent in your marketing and a group of business owners cheering you on, what could be better?

It's not about taking perfect action every time, it's about being messy and moving forward with the creative content ideas you have. I'm really proud of our group and I surprised myself that all this time while I've been writing the prompts for the membership, I've also been writing this book.

I've loved the challenge of finding 10-minute tasks that can fit in around the rest of your day and I hope that you've been able to find that time for your business. Ten minutes might not seem long, but if you did all of these tasks over the last 90 days that's an extra 15 hours you would have spent on your business that you might not have been able to do before. 15 hours! That's amazing.

Remember you don't need to follow this book in order or work through a single task each day. Sometimes I let a random generator pick a number from 1–90 and decide which task I need to work on that morning. It also helps to turn it into a game and stop procrastinating.

Marketing your business can be fun and enjoyable and we need small business owners to show us that it's possible to be successful. Our high streets have changed a lot over the last couple of years and I hope this book will help more businesses to stick around and promote the work that they do.

If you have any suggestions for themed weeks you'd like to see please let me know. We might already have them in the membership, but if we don't I'll get to work on finding some 10-minute marketing prompts for you.

If you've enjoyed this book and you would like to come and join us in The Best 90 Days Ever online membership, visit my website www.hicommunications.co.uk. The group restarts every 90 days with new prompts each time, co-working sessions, competitions and lots of support from our community of small business owners. I also have a range of digital products and offer one-to-one coaching to help you improve your marketing and grow your business. If it's something you're interested in I'd love to chat.

Thank you again for reading.

Hannah x

Key terms

Adobe Express: An online graphic design tool from Adobe.

Analytics: Your analytics tell you key pieces of information about your social media or website such as views, followers and likes.

Canva: An online graphic design tool.

Carousel post: An Instagram grid post with more than one (and up to ten) images.

Email sequence: A series of emails that would be automatically sent in order once someone joins your email list.

Engagement: The ways your audience can interact with your content or how you can start a connection with them.

Favicon: The small image that displays on your internet tab when you visit a website.

Forest app: A productivity app which encourages you to stop picking up your phone.

Hex code: The numbered code used to identify different colours.

Instagram stories: These can be found at the top of your Instagram page when you click on your profile picture circle. They last for 24 hours unless you save them to your highlights.

Launching: Talking specifically about an area of your business for a set amount of time.

Lead magnet: Something that could encourage someone to sign up for your newsletter. It's usually a freebie they would receive once they have entered their email address.

Listicle: An article made up of a numbered list.

Live: A video which is live and not pre-recorded.

Pinterest: Similar to a search engine where you can find lots of great pins full of images, recipes, blog posts and more.

Reels: A short form video that you can find on Instagram.

Search engine optimization (SEO): Improving your website so that more people can find it from a search engine.

Trello: An online project management tool that is great for storing your social media content.

Voxer: A walkie talkie app where you can text and voice note with others.

Welcome email: The first email that they would receive when they sign up to your email list.

Index

A quick word from Practical Inspiration Publishing...

We hope you found this book both practical and inspiring – that's what we aim for with every book we publish.

We publish titles on topics ranging from leadership, entrepreneurship, HR and marketing to self-development and wellbeing.

Find details of all our books at: www.practicalinspiration.com

 Did you know...

We can offer discounts on bulk sales of all our titles – ideal if you want to use them for training purposes, corporate giveaways or simply because you feel these ideas deserve to be shared with your network.

We can even produce bespoke versions of our books, for example with your organization's logo and/or a tailored foreword.

To discuss further, contact us on info@practicalinspiration.com.

Got an idea for a business book?

We may be able to help. Find out more about publishing in partnership with us at: bit.ly/PIpublishing.

Follow us on social media...

@PIPTalking

@pip_talking

@practicalinspiration

@piptalking

Practical Inspiration Publishing

Printed in the USA
CPSIA information can be obtained
at www.ICGtesting.com
JSHW051911160224
57534JS00007B/11